D1239290

PRAISE FOR *THE LIONESS IN WINTER*

"*The Lioness in Winter* speaks to pain, illness, reflection, and even suicide. Given the author's experience as a researcher—once a middle-aged scholar who believed in the texts that we use to train the next generation of gerontologists—her perspective is particularly well informed. She has not only taught it, but now lives it. She writes from a unique and important vantage point."
Kate de Medeiros, Miami University

"A lovely book, and not only because of the writers Burack-Weiss quotes. The writer describes her own experience of aging, and she takes inspiration from women who are old, bruised, and brilliant, aflame with words. I read the book pen in hand, keyboard nearby—so I could get down lines I need to remember, books I long to read."
Arlene Heyman, author of *Scary Old Sex: Short Stories*

"A slim beautiful volume that is part memoir, part career-confessional, but most compellingly a collection of writings on aging from women [Burack-Weiss] admires."
East Hampton Star

"Filled with warmth, wisdom, and knowledge, Burack-Weiss's work eloquently encourages dialogue and understanding about the inner and outer life of aging women."
Publisher's Weekly, **starred review**

"Lovely....Encouraging....*The Lioness in Winter* is the story of one person's effort to know and give value to herself as an old woman—a person with intellectual curiosity and the ability to accept change with equanimity."
Women's Review of Books

"A wonderfully enlightening and important read about what lies ahead."
Bellevue Literary Review

"The narrative experience is ripe with the inchoate newness of the past: the words of a variety of women waiting rediscovery as Burack-Weiss applies them to her life. This is the gift manifest in The Lioness.
The Gerontologist

OLD WOMAN AND THE CITY

ANN BURACK-WEISS

Published in 2022 by
Bridge Builder Press
47 Cleveland Street
Orange, NJ 07050

ISBN: 9798218032920

A Publication of the Maggie INK Project

The publishing of this book, *Old Woman and the City*, has been
made possible by the support of the Maggie INK Project. This
Project was established at the University of Orange by co-founder Maggie
Thompson. Maggie published her own memoir, *From One to Ninety-One:
A Life,* when she was 91. She said the writing of that book was, "…a rescue
of my life. I crave this for other people who are poor or elderly. If you just
start writing, you will feel better."

Cover and Interior design by Keith Kinsella for Tiger Paw Design.
Cover photography: Keith Kinsella

BRIDGEBUILDER PRESS
publishing in **New Jersey** since 1976

DEDICATION

For Grandmothers
Fannie Lander Burack
Rose Tuck Levinson

For Granddaughters
Danielle C. Nelson
Jennie Rose Nelson

ACKNOWLEDGMENTS

To be old is to understand, as never before, that "independent living" is an oxymoron; that indebtedness to others can never be overestimated or repaid. So these acknowledgments are the briefest recognition of those to whom I offer thanks.

The interdisciplinary QRM writing group — founded at Columbia in the mid-90s by Adolph Christ and Mindy Fullilove — has been my writing home for over 20 years. Members come and go, "pages" come and go, but the essentials—kindness, respect for process, nuanced critiques–remain unchanged. Current participants who have offered invaluable insight in the development of this book are John Kavanaugh, Simon Fortin, Jim Gilbert, Kelli Harding, Vivian (Didi) Heller, Kim Hill, Craig Irvine, Jack Saul, Robert Sember, and Maura Spiegel.

Those whose words and writings on the aging process that have influenced my own include Julia Ballerini, Sandra Buechler, Heather Cariou, Rita Charon, Jane Seskin, Amy Schaffer. Ann Wyatt.

I am honored to be published by the Maggie INK project of the University of Orange and Bridgebuilder Press. And deeply grateful to Mindy Fullilove for years of encouragement. This book would remain in bits and pieces on my computer if not for the thoughtful editorial counsel of Susan Hasho and skilled production aid of Keith Kinsella and Kevin Kinsella.

Special thanks to Baylis Greene of the *East Hampton Star*, unknown editors of Metropolitan Diary in *The New York Times*, and the late, Ronni Bennett of *Time Goes By* who published early versions of some of these essays.

For Roy Weiss of blessed memory, for our descendants Donna Nelson, Kenneth Weiss, Danielle Nelson, Jennie Rose Nelson and our "children of another mother" Chris Kohan and Liz Tuccillo, all the love a heart can hold.

By a Departing Light
Emily Dickinson

By a departing light,

We see acuter, quite,

Than by a wick that stays.

There's something in the flight

That clarifies the sight

And decks the rays.

TABLE OF CONTENTS

STARTING OUT

KEEPING ON

MOVING TO

STARTING OUT

WHAT WOULD HAPPEN

What would happen if one woman told the truth about her life?
The world would split open.
—Muriel Rukeyser

I doubt Muriel Rukeyser was thinking of an octogenarian's life or believed that one person could affect seismic change. More likely, she trusted that the toxic influences of a patriarchal society would appear in any story of intimate, business, or social relationships a woman might tell; that one story would invite others, that once the ball got rolling there was no telling where it might end.

Rukeyser did not live to see the Me-Too movement but would not have been surprised—so firmly did she believe in the power of long-silenced voices to break through barriers that once seemed impermeable.

But what if you are long past the days of Me Too, workplace discrimination, the male gaze, the marriage plot, the empty nest? What if you are now at a time of life when most challenges are not caused by the patriarchy but by age itself? Changes in your appearance, health, capacity to care for yourself; illnesses and deaths of those you hold most dear, riding a seesaw of hope and fear as you face your own last days.

That was me at the age of 74; mourning the death of Roy, the love of my life for over half a century, facing other losses wherever I turned. I had been practicing, teaching, and writing about old people for decades yet felt as unprepared as someone who had never given the idea of old age a second thought.

The life writing of women who had walked the road before me offered hope.

Many (Edith Wharton, MFK Fisher, Colette, May Sarton) were a generation or two older. Several (Alix Kates Shulman, Adrienne Rich, Joan Didion) were contemporaries. A few (Mary Gordon, Nancy Mair) were Baby Boomers, a generation behind.

Reading of the way these women created meaning out of their daily lives prodded me to look at my own life differently. I copied down quotes that spoke to my condition. I responded with writing about all that their words had given rise to within me. Fragments grew into chapters. Chapters grew into a book. Six years later, *The Lioness in Winter: Writing an Old Woman's Life* was published in hardcover; the paperback followed in 2017. Many readers felt inspired by the quotes I had unearthed, by my attempt to apply them to my life.

I was 80 years old by then and it looked as if I had said all I had to say about living with loss in late life. Why then did I keep on writing? It seems as if I had taken on the confidence of the Lionesses; the belief that whatever they had to say mattered.

Their self-assurance was justified. Publishers were ready, legions of readers poised for what they had to say next. That no one was waiting to hear from me was not a deterrent, it was a stimulant. Not only was I freed from the constraints of academic publication but—and this came as a great surprise—I no longer needed the Lionesses' words to get me going. The training wheels were off and I was spinning off on my own power, far off the block into new regions.

Looking around the loft I had shared with Roy for twenty-seven years and lived in by myself for nine. Taking in the sights and sounds of New York, my beloved, adopted city. Re-visiting in spirit, and occasionally in person, the Montauk that had been our family retreat for decades. Walking down avenues and streets that held memories of fifty years of professional practice. The present and past alive in me, spilling onto page after page.

I girded myself for changes ahead. Some were predictable—slippages of my own functioning; more serious losses of contemporaries. Then came 2020. Downsizing from what I thought would be my last place to a small, more manageable apartment was stressful in itself. I could not have expected that a 14-month COVID lockdown would follow within a month of the move. A changed life in many ways but one—writing the truth of my old woman's life had become a necessity.

I am not coy about my age; I sometimes volunteer it when no one has asked. Not because I expect anyone to be amazed at the number (no one has yet remarked that they imagined me to be younger) but because I myself am amazed to have lived so long, still putting one foot in front of the other, grateful for each day.

Now that COVID restrictions are cautiously being lifted and we are back on the streets again, I see reflections of myself (including nonagenarians and ounger Baby Boomer sisters) everywhere.

There she is ahead of me on the sidewalk, walking at a good pace though she may slow suddenly to look in a window causing me to stop short to avoid a collision. Sometimes she is making her way with a cane or walker that I have to navigate around. (If it is one of my cane days, we nod in silent commiseration.) She sits in the booth across from mine at the restaurant asking the waitperson to please repeat the specials. Or two seats down on the park bench or at the movie where she (like me) has come early to snare her favorite seat. She is ahead of me on the check-out line, taking a bit too long to get her purchases on the counter, the money out of her purse. She probably lives by herself or with an aging partner, family and friends within calling distance, but most often alone. She is not seriously ill nor is she in blooming health. She will have good days and bad days until there are no more days. She will then be gone but her place will soon be filled. The steady stream of old women shows no signs of abating any time soon.

What thoughts accompany her? What of the past lives on in her present? How does she envision her future? And, come to think of it, exactly what does she do with herself all day? Her story might help the generations behind her as they climb the ladder of time; it might inspire her contemporaries to reflect on their own lives, to see their own potential. It might inspire every one of every age to question the silence.

It is a deep silence. The old woman's voice is hushed by the fear and distaste of younger people for a preview of their own decline, a reminder of their own mortality, and by her own degrading of what she has to offer. "I'm just an ordinary person, nothing special to report," I hear her say.

My life, like hers, is still in the making. On these pages I share my lived experience in all its ordinariness. What if it prompts another old woman to speak into the recorder, pick up the pen, sit down at the computer and tell her story. What if another, and another, and another old woman follows? What would happen?

ONLY IN NEW YORK

It is the summer of 2000, and I am leaving the cafeteria of The Metropolitan Museum of Art with my 10-year-old granddaughter, Dani. She is visiting from San Diego, loudly proclaiming her excitement with everything seen and heard for the first time. Her comments are warmly endorsed by the friendly cashier, a young man in an androgynous pant suit, a bangle bracelet, and a hint of eyeliner. We walk away. I am silently applauding The Met for its progressive dress code when Dani, dramatically lowers her voice to whisper, "Only in New York."

And I am back in 1946 Boston, my 10-year-old self listening to Grand Central Station on my bedside radio. I know the introduction by heart and recite along with the announcer: "Grand Central Station, crossroads of a million private lives, gigantic stage on which are played a thousand dramas daily."

When I recently heard the program's dramatic opening on YouTube, I was not surprised at forgetting what preceded that speech; an introduction to the train itself (pounds of steel, its speed and sureness of direction, "like an arrow") would not have interested me then any more then than it does now. I waited for the stories—people unknown to each other whose lives were changed by being in that place at that time.

The idea of "a private life" (Was that what I was living, all alone in my dark bedroom?) open to the meeting of strangers (a "crossroads" is what they called it) and what happened after that. The stories were not particularly memorable—boy meets girl, mild mysteries. What jolted me was the idea that I belonged in that place of possibility and chance encounters.

Listening to that show was not a secret pleasure (no one cared what I listened to) but a deeply personal one. So, each time an adult, groping for the words to define an unusually crowded space, would finally settle upon "It was like Grand Central Station," I would be startled: How could they have hit upon my heart's desire?

It is not uncommon for children to fantasize that they have been born to the wrong family, that a mistake was made and that they should have had different parents. But I have not read of that persistent idea of being born in the wrong place. I recoil from likening it to the sense of having been born in the wrong body that I have heard from some in the LGBTQ community. Their pain is so much deeper, the road to correction infinitely harder, the stigma unknown to me. But I have never heard from anyone else that sense of living the wrong life while the right life was waiting for them somewhere else, the relief of coming out of darkness into light that I felt on coming to New York City at the age of 22, at continuing here at the age of 85, and of all the years between.

I could not have imagined that—working in an advertising agency in the late 50s—I would meet the producer of Grand Central Station. Or that in the early 70s—as a community social worker—I would meet the designer of the famed Celestial Ceiling. He regaled me with tales of life on that tall scaffold, surrounded by artists of many nationalities as they installed the 12 zodiac constellations; the exhilaration of life up there amid the planets. Perhaps not enough drama for an entire episode of Grand Central Station but surely enough to hint at the promise of coincidence in which the city lives up to its hype.

"Only in New York" is a trope that has gained popularity in the past few decades—appearing in movies, songs, podcasts, Instagram messages, and even a Board Game. Metropolitan Diary, a weekly feature of the *New York Times*, carries on the message of the city's exceptionalism—with an emphasis on subway stories, strange sights, random acts of kindness.

"Here is New York" is the title of E.B. White's tribute to the city, written in 1948 and periodically exhumed and dubbed its quintessential love letter. I re-read that essay every decade or so; each time the gulf between the city he memorialized and the one I was living in growing larger. It is only now, at the last reading, that I pause at the confidence in the title "Here is New York." As if White has scooped up the city, wrapped it in his finest words and is making a gift of it to you. As if any two stories of the city could be the same.

No one has yet matched the grace or prescience of that essay; nor would any one today speak of those on the Bowery as "drunks" or divide the city into "units"—small neighborhoods of like individuals with minimal interaction beyond their borders.

If COVID19 has taught the city anything, it is that the fates of all who live here are intertwined; that though each self is a unique combination of genes and circumstances, it is housed in a body that holds the same basic components as that of all other 19 million city residents—a body that is vulnerable to disease and death, to the vagaries of politics and chance.

White wrote, "No one should come to New York to live unless he is willing to be lucky." I came to New York willing to be lucky, and I was. It was here I met the people I was meant to meet, did the things I was meant to do. Here I lived through the trials and joys of marriage and motherhood, found my tribe, my profession, my life. So even though years of living and working among the unlucky checks my pride and saddens my spirit, I rejoice.

BECOMING ONE OF THEM

New York City: 1969. The Vietnam war was raging, the civil rights movement had morphed into Black Power, the city was bankrupt, student protests were closing down universities, neighborhoods were crumbling, drug use was up, mental hospitals were emptying patients into the streets.

A perfect time to enter the Columbia School of Social Work! I was 33, both my children were in school all day, and I couldn't wait to start field work. I expected to be placed with abused children or drug using teenagers or mentally ill adults; to make a small dent in righting the wrongs of the world.

I was assigned to Older Persons Service of the Community Service Society. The average clients were in their mid-80s! What could one possibly do with, or for, anyone that old? They wouldn't get better. They would soon die. Maybe it was friendly visiting, but it wasn't Real social work, was it?

Mrs. F. was my first client. She lived in a housing project way up and way over on the East Side. The halls were filthy, the elevator stopped between floors, and I was a wreck before she even opened the door. She was 87, heavy set, wobbly on her feet as she stood there in the barest living room I'd ever seen. And angry. Why did it take us so long? The agency had promised help months ago, but they had forgotten her. No one has any use for old people. Oh no, I said, and launched into an explanation of how her name had been on a list waiting for a social work intern (me) to pick up.

I thought I had done quite well as I wrote it all up in a process note for my supervisor. So I was surprised to hear that I had completely missed the boat. "You are not there to reassure her" my supervisor said. "She is telling you how she feels. Listen."

OH. *I was supposed to Listen!* And maybe imagine how it felt to be her, alone in those bare rooms? Help promised. No one coming. Feeling forgotten.

With Mrs. F, I began learning what social workers do. She needed so much it was hard to know where to begin. Visits to the medical clinic at Metropolitan Hospital across the street had stopped as she got exhausted waiting and they never helped. She wasn't eating well as the next-door neighbor who had done the shopping couldn't continue. Her broken-down orthopedic shoes needed to be replaced but the store was far and there was no one to take her.

I brought in home care, meals on wheels, set up long overdue medical appointments. I listened. In between stories of her hard life (a Polish immigrant, abandoned by her husband, work for 30 years cleaning the rat cages in a research lab) she lamented the lack of a large metal pail to soak her large, gnarled feet. She had sent the aide out to get one, but all she came back with was a small, plastic dishpan. How Mrs. F. longed for that pail.

So it was that early on a November Sunday, our family set off for a stroll through the Lower East Side to enjoy the bounty of vendors and foods. We had just started out when I spotted a pile of just those pails in front of a hardware store. I did not yet know that there was a hardware store on every other block and that every one of them had a pile of those pails in front. I bought the first I saw. Roy, the children, and I took turns through the day toting the light but unwieldy "old lady's pail" around with us.

I will never forget Mrs. F's look of wonder and joy. Then her words. "You think of me even when you're not in the place." What it meant to her to occupy space in my mind!

The basic need to be Seen, Heard, Remembered, in each of us—heightened in old age when there is no one left to give back an image of ourselves.

I had half a dozen clients more, each embedded in memory.

Mr. K. up in Washington Heights who had just lost his wife after a siege with cancer. I went up there to help him move to his son's place upstate. At every meeting, he relived her last days in the hospital. She was strapped down because she kept pulling out the tubes. They told him it had to be that way, it was for her own good, but she kept crying "Morris, untie my hands."

"I should have untied her hands." He said that at every visit.

The lasting effect of our words and actions. How we can think we are doing good while doing unimaginable harm.

Ms. V., a retired schoolteacher with advanced cancer who was studying Spanish to speak to the building staff in their own language. She had tacked a map of the world on the wall to locate unfamiliar places mentioned in the news. Every bit of her person and her apartment scoured to a degree I could not imagine possible given her pain. I could easily imagine her caring, curiosity, and rigor in the classroom. Her phrase: "Must do is a good master."

There is an enduring self—an ageless self—within each old person that meets new situations as it did old ones.

Mrs. H., who Knew Hitler. Personally. Everyone in her set did. She had expected to grow old in Germany as generations of her Protestant family had. She and her husband were alarmed at the way things were going and spoke out. They were warned to stop talking. (How, she asked me, could you not say bad things about Hitler?) They emigrated to New York with their young

OLD WOMAN AND THE CITY

son and rebuilt their lives. Mrs. H. was now 99. Her husband had died. Her son had died. All their relatives, all their friends had died. But she had her eyes, her mind, her books. She re-read *Vanity Fair* every ten years. "You can give this book to a young girl starting out. You can give this book to an old man who has seen everything. All of life is in this book."

How right she was. I reread *Vanity Fair* every ten years. Each time it is a different book.

Maybe it is unnecessary to say that after the year was over and I got placed in what had been my dream—a community mental health center—I longed to get back to Older Persons Service. My first job; it lasted for 4 years.

Practice was different as a worker. Dozens of cases. Old men and women of every socio-economic class, every race, and ethnic group. Many health conditions: arthritis and dementia foremost but also heart disease. Diabetes, low vision, hearing loss, heart disease, cancer. Then there were fractures following falls. How many said, "Everything was fine until I had that fall."

Their one commonality—they had outlived their resources. Many had drained their financial or health resources; mostly, they were fresh out of people. Those they had cared for, who had cared for them, had passed on. The agency—me—was all they had.

My clients were scattered all over the city—some in vermin-infested hovels, a few in elegantly appointed apartments; many in rooms that were furnished with care once upon a time, now in disrepair. Public housing projects on the fringes of the city, SROs or "welfare hotels" on the Upper West Side and the East 20s. A few up in Harlem, in now-decrepit, once-grand old buildings ("The doormen wore white gloves," I am constantly told.) The former maids or nannies in walk-ups in Yorkville. Gay men in Chelsea and the Village.

Visiting the toughest neighborhoods first thing in the morning—8:00 or 9:00 am—the safest time. Entering the buildings—the creaky elevators (Does that alarm bell work? Would anyone come?) climbing flights of stairs, imagining the closed doors on either side suddenly opening, hands pulling me in (How long would it take to find me?).

The relief of spotting my clients, sometimes outside their apartment doors, more worried about my safety in the building than of their own. Choosing the hard, wood chair (nothing to crawl out) facing the door (alert to who or what could come in). Every now and then there was an intake when I thought the client lived alone, then a rumble from outside the room. I would wait. A rat, a boarder, a son who looks a bit.... not right...appearing in the doorway?

Worse than the fear were the smells. The ammonia smell that rises from the incontinent, the minty smell meant to cover the breath of alcoholics, decaying food. Worst of all, the very worst, that gag-inducing smell that rises from unwashed bodies, unwashed sheets.

My judgment was challenged at every turn. The hoarder, the smoker, the demented woman who wandered the halls of her apartment building in her nightgown and sometimes left a stove light on. All of them thought they were doing just fine when any objective viewer could see that they were not. Thoughts of them kept me up at night. How to balance Ms. P's right to self-determination with her neighbors' right to safety. How to honor Mr. J's wish to befriend the distressed young woman who followed him home from the bank and protect him from exploitation.

Then there was the granddaughter of slaves who I helped to integrate an upscale Episcopalian Residence for the Aged. (Administration was eager. She was eager. I was afraid of the push back she would face from the residents.) Hours spent in her crowded walk up, role playing what she might face, how she might respond. Moving day when she introduced me to everyone as her daughter. Was she trying to get a rise out of them, or did she really feel that way? Maybe both. She did just fine.

I kept learning, kept coming up short. Like the day I walked into Ms. L's apartment preoccupied with some small matter—a payment of hers that had not gone through—and started the session with "I have bad news." The color drained from her face. She looked as if she was about to faint. How did I not anticipate her thoughts would go to a catastrophic loss?

Slow down before entering the space of an old person living alone. Adjust your words to match their pace and understanding.

Fast forward four years and I was working in a long-term care facility (including what would now be called independent living, assisted living, nursing home.). It was the first time I met family caregivers. Heard their stories of ambivalence, of pain; saw siblings separated for years reliving old unresolved issues in the care of an aged father; saw middle-aged judges and surgeons still trying to gain approval from mothers who no longer recognized them.

There, starting out as a field instructor and knowing—with my first student as I did with my first client—that this was work I was born to do.

Over 30 years at my alma mater, Columbia School of Social Work, teaching and advising in all fields of practice but specializing in aging and caregiving. Getting my Ph.D. there at the age of 54; giving me the confidence and credibility to write, to consult, to design and lead programs and staff-development workshops while keeping a small private practice. Activities I continue (in a very modified way) today.

By the mid-90s, the gulf between the literature I was supposed to assign to students (quantitative studies and theoretical articles) and the lived experience of aging undergone by clients and their caregivers was widening. The only place I could find a reflection of a real person going through a profoundly important life experience was in memoir.

I began reading memoirs, assigning them to my students, and eventually writing two books based on what I had learned from the authors. For I had, by then, become one of them.

In *Intoxicated by My Illness and Other Writings on Life and Death*, Anatole Broyard suggests (and I paraphrase here) that you need to develop a style for your illness to keep from falling out of love with yourself; that hanging on to and building on the story of who you once were is necessary to accepting who you now are.

True of illness, true of advanced age. The cumulative effects of loss; the inevitable diminishment of all that the world might have valued in you, that you valued in yourself, threatens to drain that love.

Old women I had known in practice, old women I only knew from print, helped me hold on. They accompanied me from what I thought would be my last places on earth—the city loft, the family house in Montauk—to where I am now. A small apartment. No more the large cabinets and pantry stuffed with all that is needed to prepare large dinners, just enough to entertain two or three others. No more the Montauk garden but a table of blooming plants. Beautiful sunsets from the west windows. The Empire State building and Hudson Yards out the north. My two rooms are filled with light even on the darkest days. Visitors often remark on the absence of blinds or curtains; extol the virtue of shades that would preserve the light and protect my privacy. They don't understand my need for unfiltered light from my windows on the world.

Best of all—the bustle of 14th Street. Always something going on. If I awaken at 3:00 am, I can watch folks heading in and out of the 24-hour diner across the street. Up at dawn, I see filled trays in the windows of the Donut Pub; early risers enter empty handed and exit clutching a coffee in one hand and a white paper bag in the other. Where have they come from? Where are they going?

Life. And I am still in it.

KEEPING ON

AH, THE LONELY PEOPLE

I am seated on a bench overlooking the Hudson River on a clear autumn day. The air smells of salt. The clouds are a floating mass of foam. Sounds of children playing mingle with those of passenger boats on the water. I am savoring the scene when I am approached by a middle-aged man with a weird contraption strapped to his forehead: a large, white, rectangular cardboard box with a camera lens at the center. He asks if I would like to take a look.

The scene is the same but technically enhanced. The river and sky shimmer and keep changing color. The sounds are subsumed under a wave of strings playing New Age music. I hastily pass it back and say, "It looks like an LSD trip." He laughs more than my response warrants, adds that there are "no side effects" and goes on to show me the smartphone app from which it emanates. Before walking away, he says that he used to be alone in the park. "Now people want to talk to me."

My walk takes me past a vacant lot filled with trash, bounded on one side by a graffiti- covered building wall and three sides by chain link fencing. There is a small wooden weather-beaten sign tacked on the 2nd Avenue side: "There is no one like you." Stuck at intervals into the rusted fence are decaying bunches of dried flowers.

I see many old women pushing small dogs in baby carriages. (Or perhaps there are carriages made for dogs?) The dogs and/or the carriages are often beribboned. On buses or park benches, the dogs are removed and cuddled, often spoken to, replaced gently with a smile.

I am reading my Kindle in the ophthalmologist's waiting room and the old man seated next to me asks how it works. Before I can answer, he volunteers that he has no time for it now. He is 84, a lawyer, still working full time; a specialist in trusts and estates who has published four books. All in less than a minute!

* * *

Home alone I replay the sights and sounds of my days. I wonder how many people the man with the box found to talk to. What would inspire someone to plead his anonymous love in such a dismal space. Do the dogs sleep in their owner's beds? Sit at their tables? (Is it even correct to speak of "owners"?)

And could it be that what sounded like shameless self-promotion in the doctor's office was a geriatric pickup line?

Scenes of such naked need used to scare me. It felt as if all the loneliness, all the fears of invisibility I held within me burst out and found shape and voice in unknown others. As if all the stored-up love in the world, all the longing for connection, could not be contained.

Which is, I finally realized, as it should be. I am not a mere observer of these scenes, I am a participant. I am the strangers' "other" as surely as they are mine. I am there to accord attention to their lives, and, in so doing, extending the boundaries of my own.

* * *

> *Ah, Look at all the lonely people*
> *Where do they all come from?*
> *All the lonely people*
> *Where do they all belong?*
> "Eleanor Rigby" The Beatles

It was 1966. The Beatles wrote those lyrics when they were in their twenties, surrounded by adoring crowds. I was just a few years older, cocooned in a mesh of family and friends.

Still, they noticed. Eleanor Rigby picking up rice in a church where a wedding has been. Father McKenzie writing a sermon that no one will hear.

I played the album with that song on it many times. The opening words sounded to me—and continued to sound until I saw them in print— "I look at all the lonely people." But no, it opens with a sigh: "Ah look at all the lonely people!" I love that Ah. And bless them; the two who have died, the two who grow old along with me. So wise they were to recognize—in the midst of bountiful lives—the essential self within, the links that bind us together, and the special reward of bearing witness.

OFTEN BUT A LITTLE AT A TIME

"It's a funny thing now; I very often think of my poor wife, but I cannot think of her very much at any one time," says old Mr. Swann in Proust's *Remembrance of Things Passed*. His observation is prompted by a walk through his garden on a glorious spring day; the sight and fragrance of Hawthorn trees in bloom all-the-more wonderful when shared with a dear friend. Then he realizes that experiencing pleasure may be viewed as unseemly in the recently bereaved. And explains a phenomenon familiar to many who live on after the death of a life partner. Thoughts of them are as ephemeral as soap bubbles—floating through the present moment, evaporating as soon as we reach out to them.

Roy and I have long visits in that past where he lives in his constructions of wood and steel, in the recipe box where the directions for a six-layered wedding cake are written in his elegant, printed hand, in his favorite sweatshirt that warms me on the coldest day.

M. Swann's observation is different. We are not as we were then. We are as we are now.

I open the cabinet in which I store cookware and a large frying pan cover falls on my slippered foot. Roy stacked in the order of size. I stacked for convenience—large, frequently used vessels often teetering upon small. Big toe, right foot throbs; but I quickly realize it will be okay.

Roy appears. His facial expression what it always was when this happened—concern, relief, resignation, bemused affection for my stubbornness. He disappears. It is not his moment. He has no new moments.

If he stayed, he would wonder about that small rectangular box on the counter that even now is vibrating and letting out a mild hum. I would have to explain the Smartphone. Then Twitter. Then Trump?

No, he does not want to, need, to know. And I, like old M. Swann, need him to stop in often and stay as long as he can.

THE PALMER METHOD

My seat is by a huge window with an unobstructed view of the Empire State Building. A steady stream of people pass by. I guess which are tourists, which natives, which new immigrants.

Light as it is, the MAC Airbook has become heavy in my backpack—too heavy to cart to the coffee shop. On my right and left are people on computers, many with earphones. They fuss with chargers. Seated here with pen and pad, I feel superior; everyone knows that the greatest literature of all time was written by hand!

Nice to be able to place alternate words atop each other—to come back and select the best one later. Fun drawing brackets around sentences, arrows to indicate where paragraphs can be transposed. Once home, I can barely read my writing. Cramped fingers rushing to keep up with racing thoughts have led to elisions here, indecipherable scribbles there.

Penmanship was my best subject at the Harriet A. Baldwin School in 1945 Boston. An alphabet of perfect letters (Capital A, small a; Capital B, small b....) crawled above the blackboard in every classroom. And wasn't it called the "Palmer Method?"

Google brings this: The Palmer Method of cursive writing was devised at the end of the 19th century by Austin Palmer and held sway in public education in the U.S. for over half a century. It is not about the fingers. It is about the whole arm. It is about rhythm. Its key characteristic is muscle movement.

Isn't muscle memory at work when we remember how to ride a bike decades after the last time we attempted it? And rhythm. Isn't rhythm about cadence, the narrative voice that separates one piece of writing from another? The very essence of style. Seems I'm on to something here.

Next day at the coffee shop I warm up with long-forgotten, newly remembered push-pulls and ovals. The push-pulls are straight close together lines tilting right, the ovals are interlocking spirals. To create them, you place your elbow on the table, grip the pen, slide your fourth finger and pinky along with it and glide them onto the page. This is known as "a forearm sweep."

The shapes look as weird and magical as they always did. As if I have created and am now interpreting my own ink blot test. This day they recall a field of wheat and bales of hay. From whence this rural imagery in the middle of Manhattan?

A few people walk by my table, idly glance at my page, then at me. Doodling? Demented? I move on to letters. I do the whole alphabet before I start writing for the day. My handwriting is perfect, the letters just like the ones on Palmer's chart. Each word is legible, but the thoughts that had rushed through quicker than I could catch them are now slow in coming. So slow and banal that I give up after an hour and head home.

Still intrigued by the method, I return to Google and learn that a public education debate has been raging between cursive and printing enthusiasts for several decades now. And then.... a pop-up ad. A picture of Hillary Clinton—her face distorted in a grimace below which is copy decrying her use of a private email server. Followed by an equally unflattering picture of AOC and a diatribe against her. An algorithm has brought me here, the Opinion Page of *The Federalist*. There is nothing about penmanship on the page, but the message is clear—an interest in the Palmer Method equals conservatism in its current incarnation.

I get it! For all its graceful hoops and loops, Austin Palmer's method was designed in the spirit of the social reformers of his day. Muscle movement was about muscular self-reliance. Rhythm was learning to think the same thoughts and write the same things in the same time as those seated around you.

It all rushes back. Rows of wooden desks bolted to their seats; each bolted to the floor. The round hole that held the inkwell. The fountain pen with its steel pointed tip. The teacher asking one of the "big boys" in the back of the room to unfurl the maps that are rolled up beneath the letters. The maps of America with its "amber fields of grain" and "fruited plains." (Perhaps my earlier association with push-pulls and ovals?) There are no people on the maps, I had escaped to New York for just that reason.

Next day I return to the coffee shop without pen or pad. The Mac book no longer feels quite so heavy. I take it from its case, plug it in, and begin to write.

DRESSING FOR BED

There was a time in my life when dressing for bed became dressing for a lover. Because it was the 1950s and I was a bride from Boston, the lover was a husband. And because Boston brides of the day had not heard of black lace teddies, the hottest thing going was a peignoir set: silk, voluminous from neck to ankle, trimmed with satin bands and trailing bows. They came in virginal white, baby pink, and baby blue. You might have seen one in movies of the day. She was wearing one as she kissed him chastely on the cheek, carefully removed the robe, draped it over the foot of her bed, and climbed in. Then he got into his bed, leaned over, and shut off the lamp on the table between them. Although their bedtime didn't resemble ours, the very act of encasing oneself within those frothy layers (often accompanied by a pair of satin backless slippers known as "mules") lent a touch of Hollywood glamor to the evening's activities.

After four years and two children, the peignoir set gave way to summer cotton and winter flannel—punctuated by short, silky "nighties" made for fun. What ever happened to my trousseau collection? The last time I remember wearing a set was as a joke—on a 10th anniversary weekend at the St. Regis hotel. It was the sixties, after all.

Now that I am a widow in my eighties, I still dress up for bed. My breasts don't wobble about but are firmly secured in a lightweight cotton bra. I wear well-cut cotton underpants as well—over which will be one of many outfits I have deemed appropriate for the occasion. Perhaps a long T shirt. Perhaps well-tailored jersey and sweatpants. My costume is lightweight, brightly colored, perhaps patterned with stripes or flowers.

I think of the poem "Warning"—published in 1961 immortalized in greeting cards, magnets, coffee mugs, wall plaques, and international women's groups ever since; its author, Jenny Joseph, voted the United Kingdom's most popular poet in a 1996 poll by the BBC. Somewhere along its road to fame, the poem acquired an accompanying picture—a grey-haired, toothless old crone in a crumpled cap, wearing a look of demented glee. Generations of readers now recognize that first line "When I am an Old Woman, I Shall Wear Purple." —the "I" being a convention-bound woman in mid-life longing to act in outrageous ways and looking forward to a time when she would be free to be her true self.

But what if you continue to be your true self and it is the world that has changed?

I find old age like a dream where you think you are in a new country until you realize that the country is the same but your place in it has changed. No longer at the center, you are on the periphery. A bit player in other people's lives. So, dressing for bed has become more than I originally intended. It is now, my way of enlarging the picture.

Amour Propre. It sounds better in French. Love of oneself that is not unbridled narcissism but self-respect. At a time of life when so much in the world seems bent on seeing me as diminished, less than, not worthy of, dressing for bed is a way of saying, "I am still me. "

After many washings, my night-time wardrobe is now as thin and faded as the body within. Replenishment is needed. I take myself off to a major department store. I ask the young greeter at the door where I can find "The Lingerie Department" and—after a long trek—find I have been directed to towels and linens. Do they no longer call it "lingerie?" I lose confidence but am determined and soldier on, eventually locating "Sleepwear." All has changed in the decade since I last looked.

Where is the sexy stuff? Most likely relegated to specialty shops while sleepwear—like cookware—remains for the practical shopper. There are some strange garments here. Ground-sweeping gowns with hoods. Lady lumberjack shirts of a violent plaid. Softly draped jumpsuits that look as if they could easily move from bed to gym to office and—with the addition of heels and jewelry—be fit for a night on the town. I stop at the grannie gowns. Adorable. All they really need is a tattoo to set them off. Perhaps for one of my granddaughters? After much indecision, I make two choices: a classic cotton gown with a subtle pattern of pink on white and a knee-length gray terry cloth pullover with bat wing sleeves. Once at home, I straighten out my collection and note that it is now filled with outfits fit for every mood and season. A pleasure for myself to behold.

In the movie *Sunset Boulevard*, the aged actress Norma Desmond famously says: "I am still big. It's the pictures that got small." There is no audience waiting for her appearance; her belief may be false, but the need to hold on to her former self rings true.

Like Norma, I am ready for my close-up now.

COMFORT ZONE

You'd think they'd let up by the time you reach your 80s. That all you need do to keep yourself going is to keep yourself going. But no; everything you hear or read pushes you toward new horizons.

That thrill of completion that I feel when finishing the Sunday crossword puzzle (well, all but three small words) is meaningless. It does not spark those neurons or create new pathways in the brain; all it does is deepen familiar ruts. Worse, it is a solitary pursuit. Surely social isolation and dementia are brewing in the toxic waters of my comfort zone.

Old folks are repeatedly told to heed the siren call of the untried that, from the beginning of time, has lured humans from their caves into the sun of enhanced existence. Learning Chinese would be just the thing. Or I could put aside the knitting of one color, one pattern scarves that I've enjoyed since the age of 18—an activity that is especially pleasant on long winter evenings cuddled on the couch listening to the classical music I've enjoyed just as long. Better to join a class in needlepoint. It takes lots of different colored threads to construct a tapestry—you must keep your wits about you in order to keep them sorted, threaded, and hitting just the right spot, all the while chatting with others engaged in the same task.

They mean well, the young dears. It is just that they are afraid of their own senescence. Neuroscience offers hope. And yes, I've seen the graphs, read the papers. I know enough about research to agree that the findings are statistically significant. But it's a long way from statistical significance to my apartment, to my life, where I have to say that the findings are not significant at all.

You see, we are often afraid. The unknown is only filled with wonder if you feel power within you to grab out to it and turn it to your uses.

We are afraid as young children are afraid—so much in life they don't understand, can't control. The things that hide out in the shadows and can pounce at any time are particularly scary when a child is alone in the dark. So, they ask for glass after glass of water, need to hear the same story, the same way, over and over. Skip a page in the book, change a few words, and they get upset.

Ours is not a second childhood. We know full well the names and workings of what is hiding in the shadows. We do not imagine animals escaped from the zoo to hide out under our beds (as I remember doing at the age of four), but the bed itself springing steel sides pulled up high over which tubes ferry fluids in and out of our bodies. We do not imagine that our screams won't be loud enough to reach powerful adults who can come to our aid. We know the limits of the powerful adults, no matter how caring they might be. So, like children, we cannot see change as a learning opportunity, a chance to face our fears and triumph over them. Instead, change strips us of all sense of certainty, of control, leaving us quaking in its wake; strips us of our memories and the sense of self that they reinforce within us.

The Sunday crossword puzzle I am working on today holds vestiges of every puzzle of my life, everyone who was around me on those long-ago Sundays—the places I carried it with me during the week to fill in a clue or two, the people—so many no longer here—with whom I exchanged passing references to its difficulty or ease or cleverness of theme.

Knitting the long scarf which I rip and redo as often as I move ahead, and the music that accompanies it, go all the way back to my room at home, then a college dormitory room filled with smokers and bridge players where, doing neither, I found my place and many happy hours with the knitters. Those last months of pregnancy with each of my now middle-aged children when I surprised myself by branching out to blanket, sweater, and bootie sets—enough even to gift to others

So, I'll stay right here. Comforted by the familiar, buoyed by memories. Relaxing? Lolling? No, Wallowing—that's the word I'm looking for, wallowing, in my comfort zone.

MY EULOGY

I will never be remembered as a woman of mystery, cool and polished on the outside, teeming with passions and plans within, observed by friends and colleagues as unknowable despite years of shared activities and conversations.

As a woman of mystery, I would quietly nod at remarks that please as well as those that offend—reserving comments until they could be expressed in well-crafted responses that carry a note of ambiguity. I would not have one email address spelling my name for the world to see but keep several open at once using a different pseudonym to correspond with each network.

Alas, it was not to be. Every emotion is registered on my face. Every thought finds words—spoken or translated into emails or texts, the forefinger of my right hand twitching toward "send."

I would like to be remembered as a person who worked hard at whatever came her way, who always did her best. Here intrude memories of past mistakes, errors of judgment large and small. They rankle, causing me angst decades after they occurred.

That I was not the best wife, mother, daughter, friend, worker, was never for lack of giving it my all. This is not, I know, such a great distinction. Mass murderers probably accord themselves that honor. That it was always in the service of being what I think of as "a good person" very possibly a delusion.

Roy once said he knew he had to marry me because I was so Enthusiastic! But if, like Browning's Last Mistress, I have "a heart too soon made glad" does that not speak as easily to a lack of discrimination as to an ardent spirit?

I think of my father who died suddenly of a stroke at the age of 77. In the months leading up to his death, he was legally blind, in constant pain, and could barely walk. His answer when asked how he was? "Never better." He was not being ironic. I doubt he knew the word. A seventh-grade dropout who never read a book or wrote anything longer than a sentence (a sentence that covered three pages in a large loopy hand and—unconstrained by rules of spelling or grammar and whatever the subject—had a subtext of love). My father lived for the joy he took in people. So happy was he to be in your

...pany that, to him, it must have felt like the best time he'd ever had.

My father died in 1980. There are few people now alive who remember him. But—here's the point, here's my wish—mention Bob Burack years after his death, and anyone who knew him would smile. What they said after didn't matter. It was that involuntary smile at hearing his name. As if he had just walked into the room and they were glad to see him again. I would like to be remembered by that smile.

THE MAN OF HEARTS

My father was a traveling salesman who never came back from a trip without a story. One day he spoke of meeting a buyer who sat behind his desk while they spoke. On the desk was a large white paper on which the man drew heart after heart. Inside each heart he printed "Peace and Contentment."

Why did I think someone would do something like that? I was only in second grade and the fact that he asked for my opinion was surprising. I asked question after question, as if getting the picture clear in my mind would solve the mystery. Did he draw all the hearts first and then do the printing or did he do them one by one? Was it a pad of paper or only one sheet? Was the pen red? (It seemed as if it had to be red.)

The image caught my fancy. I'd cover large sheets of paper with hearts within which I tried to fit the words—though "contentment" was really too long a word to squeeze into the bottom half of a heart.

It was hard to make head or tail of it. My father knew the man had been an alcoholic and was in AA which, we thought, might explain it. It sounded like the kind of thing that a Christian in such a group (for we knew that Jews could never become alcoholics) might be advised to do. Several other possibilities were raised and rejected before we dropped the subject.

The memory has returned to me from time to time over the years. It used to be when I saw a movie that portrayed an office scene in the 1940s. The scene is in black and white. There is a heavy phone on the mahogany desk. The men wear suits and smoke cigarettes while they talk.

Lately though, I think only of my father—not in the faraway room with the man of hearts but at the kitchen table with me. Noticing all that is strange and wonderful in the people we meet, marveling at the many ways there are to live a life, the impossibility of ever knowing why anyone does anything, the importance of trying.

A PALACE IN TIME

To grow up Jewish in Boston in the 1930s and 40s was to be perpetually "other"—squeezed between White Anglo-Saxon Protestants who dominated the outside world and Irish Catholics all around us.

Shabbat—for girls under 14—was Saturday morning service for which we prepared on Monday and Wednesday afternoons. Each year we went over the same stories, the same songs, tried again to sound out a few lines of Hebrew—just enough knowledge to prepare a young woman to take on the role of a Jewish wife.

In the year before confirmation (there were not yet Bat Mitzvahs) we sang in the Junior Choir and took turns preparing sermons on the Torah portion of the week. Released from the predictability of the school week and Sundays visiting relatives lent Saturday a special aura.

We had learned about Protestants in our first-grade reading book. The children—Dick and Jane—lived with their parents and dog Spot in a house, in Real America where people lived in houses with lawns in front, families went on picnics at the lake, and it seemed everyone had blond hair and blue eyes

Most of the Irish Catholics who surrounded us had blond hair and blue eyes too. And although they lived much as we did (in small apartments with parents who had never seen a lake or gone on a picnic) they were privileged by being the majority and by what the girls got to wear.

The lacy white dresses and veils of First Holy Communion were bride-like, beautiful. Around their necks were tiny crosses, some studded with shiny jewels, St. Christopher medals and—wonder of wonders—grains of sand encased in small transparent lockets.

So besotted was I by the jewelry that, at the age of nine, I saved up my allowance and purchased a small Jewish star on a gold chain. The face of my usually gentle uncle grew dark: "You feel your religion in your heart, you don't wear it on your chest. You look like a New York Jew."

A New York Jew was "flashy." The women wore nail polish, mink coats, big diamonds. The men drove Cadillacs. And all they cared about, spoke about, lived for, was money.

With noxious stereotypes of our tribe in a place far from us, Boston Jews defined themselves by the opposite. The successful men drove Lincolns, their wives wore coats of seal or beaver. Jewelry was conservative and no one wore makeup. We were taught to move through the world without calling attention to ourselves, to speak softly, be polite and never ever to speak of money.

Catholic was First Holy Communion dresses and enviable jewelry. Protestant was Real America somewhere far from Boston. Jewish was an identity. Jewish was latkes at Chanukah and a seder at Passover. Jewish was the horror of the holocaust and pride in the post-war founding of Israel. Jewish was prayers and songs that I repeated by rote.

I grew up and moved to New York. I met adult versions of Dick and Jane fresh from Real America, found they were less wholesome, more interesting than I could have imagined. I met a few New York Jews who fit my uncle's description but many more who didn't. Irish Catholics were in short supply but one I met became a dearest friend. Being with her always felt like home.

The vast tapestry that made up the people of the city was thrilling. The three fixed categories of being carried over from childhood gave way to variations beyond imagining. Men and women who were not either/or but both/many came into my life, into my home.

When handed a questionnaire, I continued to check "White/Non-Hispanic" in the race box and "Jewish" in the religion box; even though I had come to see race as a social construction and religion as an accident of birth.

Jewish religious rituals felt irrelevant and—after the pro forma bar mitzvah of my son and traditional funeral rites for my parents—I decided against a Jewish funeral for Roy (who had even less interest in organized religion than I). No unknown rabbi would pull phrases from the bible to describe the man I knew so long and loved so well. There was a memorial for family and close friends in our loft—the only words spoken by those he loved, those who loved him.

Then, after 60 years of living in New York, of entering one synagogue after another for a wedding, a bar mitzvah, or a funeral, I was invited to Shabbat services in a different kind of temple.

The chief rabbi was a Korean woman. Another female rabbi and her wife were preparing to welcome their first child. Other rabbis, cantors—men and women—played guitars. And sang. A small choir and instrumental group made music that rocked the sanctuary. They were the songs I had sung in the choir. The Shema was just as my father had taught me to say it when I was four years old. I remembered every word.

When we turned to wish Shabbat Shalom to those seated around us, I saw faces that didn't "look Jewish," spoke to a couple with unidentifiable accents. Klezmer music played as the Torah was carried around and congregants— waiting to touch it with prayer book or hand—chatted and danced in place. The words bound up in its scroll had been read by the Boston relatives of my childhood, the Eastern European ancestors I had never known, and who knew how many generations of ancestors before that. No sooner did I touch that Torah than I began to cry.

I still cry. Every time. I cry even as I watch the Friday night service on Zoom. I rise and sit on cue. I sing along with *Hashkiveinu* (a Prayer for Protection) and feel as if I am offering a prayer for all the world.

* * *

Once I found my way back to Shabbat I realized how much I had forgotten, how little I had ever known. I read "The Sabbath" by Rabbi Abraham Heschel who writes "the seventh day is like a palace in time with a kingdom for all. It is not a date but an atmosphere."

According to Heschel (a leading figure in Jewish intellectual life and social justice movements in the United States in the 50s and 60s) the Sabbath is a celebration of life, life that came before and will come after our brief days on earth. He writes that while Christianity finds holiness in space (I think here of Chartres) Jews honor time.

And we are given the opportunity Every Single Week (how could I have missed this?) to devote a day to appreciating living within the flow of time.

It is not meditation that witnesses thoughts as they pass and peacefully lets them go. It is not mindfulness that focuses attention on what is going on within oneself. It is not gratitude toward specific people for specific acts. It is not the serenity prayer to a Higher Power with the choice of changing or accepting the hard times that come our way.

It is not about our individual lives at all. It is a looking outside of the self and its daily rounds; a time out from life to appreciate life, and our brief time in it.

I now spend my Saturdays in purposeful celebrations of time. I may walk through the Greenmarket noting seasonal fruits and vegetables. Or listen to opera on the radio and recall Caruso and Callas who excelled in the roles in decades past and imagine that someone listening with me now will be on that stage in the future. Sometimes I sit by the Hudson River, look down to the Statue of Liberty and recall all who came to this city long before me. Then

I marvel at those walking by—most of whom were not alive when I first saw this river, the babies and children who will one day be here with their grandchildren. Often, I meet with friends. Some I've known for over 40 years. Others have come into my life in the past decade or so. All are reminders that I am a bridge between what was and what will be.

Greater minds than mine have puzzled over biblical teachings for millennia. Surely their descendants (including Heschel) would find my understanding simplistic. They might argue that each Shabbat ritual has a meaning that is glossed over in my search for an easy answer; that deeper study will deepen, broaden my faith.

Some day. Perhaps.

For now, I feel sufficient comfort in looking back. Early Shabbats that set my faith in motion, mid-life Shabbats that blew it apart, and a weekly reminder now that I am nearing my end, that as long as I draw breath, I am alive in time.

STAGING

Although the broker delivers the news tactfully, he cannot soften the impact: This apartment and all that abides within it—including me—are not fit to be seen. We are perfectly respectable, even possess a certain bygone charm. But much as one loves visiting grandmother's house, you do not want to live there.

It is easy enough to absent myself for showings. Would that I could take the furniture with me. Since it must remain in all its dated glory, a stager is brought in to "freshen it up." Everything is repositioned. Personal effects are tucked away. Pillows abound. The days of White and Faux begin. White as new fallen snow are the rugs and throws that create a winter wonderland in my living room. Faux plants are here, there, everywhere. Her work is done.

The first morning we struggle to get our bearings. Then, from the tallest of the three painted tables huddled together in front of the couch, "We thought we'd never see each other again!" The tables had come from my in-laws' apartment in Miami only to be separated on arrival. Not just separated, exiled to far corners of the room; one covered in Belgian lace and a succession of orchids, two covered with large brass plates heaped with books and whatnots. Corners now touching, their aqua surfaces shine in the sun. Curved golden legs kick a cancan of delight.

The carpet opens with a reproach. Why do I persist in calling it an Oriental rug? It is a Persian rug. And not from a factory with decent ventilation and workplace standards. It was woven by child laborers—12 hours a day of eye-straining effort. Then rolled tightly and placed on a ship to America, covering many floors before it got to mine over 30 years ago. How could I not have noticed that the underpad had begun to come apart? Such an itch! What blessed relief when the stager lady lifted a corner, discovered the problem, swept up the pieces, and laid it directly on the floor. Ah, the smooth coolness of bare wood underneath.

The second morning I find the room deep in conversation. Several pieces go way back, having emigrated together in 1980 from my parents' apartment in Boston. The dining room set, the desk, the footstool, and a few lamps remember it well. Yes, the thick, gold wall-to-wall carpet that held them was soft and comforting, but then there were the cigarettes. The air is so much clearer here!

The side chairs and wrought-iron lamps have little to say for themselves. Their memories don't go back further than West Elm. (Though the red chair, the most recent addition, does recall its beginnings in North Carolina—being packed and loaded into a truck bound for New York by burly men in MAGA caps.)

The third morning I pull a chair up to the Sheraton Desk (it prefers to be referred to by its full name). It is the finest reproduction of the finest wood and has held pride of place in many living rooms for over half a century. Two perfect little knobs grace the top, and delicate gold engraving is etched all over the stained dark wood. I make my apologies. I know it had endured three moves in Massachusetts and two in New York since then, each of them landing it where it belonged—tucked into a corner. Not in the middle of a long white wall with an ersatz cherry blossom tree nudging its lower-right corner.

I am so sorry for losing the little keys to open the top cubbyholes. I hope that saving the blotter compensates, but, of course, a blotter is not of the desk, it is on the desk. (And really too large to lose). Yes, I remember its glory days—when my mother would draw up a chair, write a letter or pay a bill with a fountain pen, and use the blotter. I assure it this move is only temporary. When I move, it will come with me. There is sure to be a corner somewhere.

The fourth morning, I hear the laughter before I enter the room. It is about the stager lady and pillows. The couch's ordeal! On with the blue, off with the blue. Maybe stripes? Big or small? Three? No, two pillows on each side? Maybe all on one side with the oversize gold one on the other?

They are deep into this when the little footstool speaks. (Where did that footstool even come from? All I know is it has been in every apartment of my life. It has survived four chairs and is now snuggled up to the couch as if it belongs there.) "How about a game? Close your eyes and guess how many 'faux' plants. Ready, get set...."

The Sheraton Desk: "Wait. Should we count only the green ones or include the white ones? And we must really differentiate between the floor ones and the table ones."

"Stop being so pedantic," says the footstool. The Sheraton Desk shuts up.

We begin to count. Not hard to correctly guess the ones on the floor—four. But the little ones are tucked into small spaces. Everywhere. Even the happy little tables have to put up with one. The numbers come up short. (Last I counted there were 14, but they seem to magically multiply when no one is looking.)

Frissons of excitement greet me on the fifth morning. This is the day the broker man plans to bring people in! The couch is full of itself. Sagging and faded for a few years, it has been granted a new lease on life. Newly festooned with colorful pillows, face-forward in a manner that showcases its curvaceous shape, it can't stop preening.

"I'm sure they'll love me," it says. "Well, I am something special too," says the Sheraton Desk, and suddenly I realize: a terrible misunderstanding. They think the people are coming to see them!

How to break the news, that the people are coming only to see the apartment, that the people might find them old-fashioned, that all the fussing was just to make them more presentable?

"You see," I begin carefully, "we have grown old together. And young people prefer what is new and sleek. In fact, the broker man has created just such a picture of our place in the advertisement. It is called a virtual room." A virtual room? They look to the Sheraton Desk for an explanation. It is as mystified as they are.

"Virtual is like—," I falter. Then go on. "Virtual is like it's not real but wanting you to imagine it is." Warmed up, I continue. "So, in the picture there are two long gray couches at right angles and a big black table. That is because long gray couches and big black tables make the people imagine that they could live here themselves. They want to make their own memories, not think about ours."

The first open house is in an hour. Time for me to go. But not without finishing what I started. "We will be moving away. I will try to bring you all with me, but some of you won't fit. And even if you come with me, it won't be forever. But we don't have to worry about that now. We'll live on together as long and as well as we can. We will have each other. We will have our old stories. We will do just fine."

COVER UP

It was the spring of 1977. I was the only child of old, sick parents I was the only mother of two angry adolescents. I was the only clinical preceptor of eight graduate students. Wherever I was, I should have been somewhere else. Whatever I did was less than was needed. I went to therapy.

The psychiatrist was a kindly man, the office was on Central Park West and there were covers on everything. Large throws atop the upholstered couch, every pillow had a sham, and it was hard to extricate a Kleenex from its wicker work casing. The bathroom had wall-to-wall carpet, a plush toilet seat cover, and the spare roll of toilet tissue wore sort of a cap—a jaunty crocheted affair with a little pompom on top.

I talked and talked about my parents, my children, my students but in the back of my mind—and even between sessions—I could not stop thinking about those covers.

Wasn't a therapist's office a place to pull off the covers, to expose what was hidden from view?

I amused myself with imagining how I might respond to the situation. "Wondering why everything is so covered up in here." Of course, he'd ask me to tell him more about it and I'd rant on and on. Nothing good could come of that.

Perhaps a subtle gaslight maneuver? Like I could take the cap off the spare roll of toilet paper and just lie it beside. He would put it back on—wondering, "did I leave it like that?" I'd wait a few weeks and then, do it again. You could really make someone crazy that way, but he was such a nice man.

Or I could do a full-scale drama scene. Channeling Joan Crawford and "no wire hangars" in Mommy Dearest, I could race through the office shouting "no more covers" and rip everything apart? No good. 911 would carry me off and then I couldn't do anything for anyone.

I continued to talk and talk about the pressures of my life but after the fourth week or so I began to bore myself. The therapist had asked few questions and offered no insights, so how did it suddenly become clear? My parents would not be around forever. My children would grow up and calm down. My students would finish their assignments and get on with their lives. I might never know the right thing to do for them or know it and not be able to do it, but I could do my best and it would have to be enough. Days would pass. Life would go on.

Forty years have passed since that last session, but I remember it well. I had prepared my script. I would thank the therapist for the patient listening that allowed me to come to an answer I could live with. And leave with a few humorous asides about the covers. I never got around to it. I cried. I struggled once again to tug a Kleenex out of its too snug wrapper. I left.

Many years later I learned that he had retired and moved to Virginia. Did he take all the covers with him?

THE GERIATRIC GAZE

I boarded the M4 bus on the coldest of winter days. I cannot say I bounded the steps with youthful alacrity, but I did pretty well—no cane or walker to assist my ascent. There was a hat pulled down over my brow, a thick scarf swaddling my neck, and I was bundled head to toe in parka, fleece-lined yoga pants, and boots fit for hiking an Alpine trail.

At first sight of me, two passengers jumped up simultaneously—as if an electrical current had just passed under their seats. Indeed, the posted sign "Please Give Your Seat to the Old or Disabled" suggested they do so. But how—even with sunglasses concealing all that nasty business around the eyes—did they know?

The sign itself—two adjectives in search of a noun—has always amused me. I picture a phalanx of the old and disabled (humans? barnyard animals? zoo creatures?) boarding the bus at once as in some dystopian movie of the end of days. What would become of the other passengers? Would the driver change the destination sign? Pull a hood and scythe out of the duffle bag that sits beside him in the huge plastic enclosure that engulfs him? And exactly what anticipated catastrophe was that enclosure designed to resist?

Such thoughts could consume a reverie the whole length of a Fifth Avenue ride. But this day was different. Something had changed. After decades of being invisible, I was seen again. The sense of emitting an electromagnetic force, a force I could neither understand nor control, recalled the time I was first seen.

It was the white latex bathing suit with the zipper up the back that did it. I wore it to the beach at Winthrop, Massachusetts, the summer I turned 15. Before that day I had spent years sunbathing or swimming at that beach, a body among a mass of unremarkable bodies. The suit changed everything. The very air around me was suddenly charged, wave upon wave of the male gaze. It was to follow as I grew older and didn't disappear for good until I reached my 50s.

I was never a beauty—and that irresistible flush of just-bloomed desirability was soon to fade—but any woman of average looks who takes reasonable care of her appearance lives in its web. And finds a way to respond.

The BBDO I entered as a young secretary was the quintessential New York advertising agency of "Mad Men." The suggestive speech that would trigger an H.R. investigation today was a matter of course; being cornered in an office or having a breast cupped from behind as your boss reached for the phone in your hand earned him the designation of "pig" and taught you how to duck and weave.

I recall only one moment of indignation on my part. I had overheard one of the senior account executives commenting to my boss on a memo "your broad sent me." Perhaps it was "your"—the implication that I was a possession of my boss. Perhaps it was "broad"—a crude degradation of all things female.

Empowered by rage, I waited until he returned to his office and was seated behind his desk, walked right in, walked right up to him, and said: "By 'your broad' did you mean me? Were you talking about me?" His response (surprise, confusion, shame, apology) affirmed that I had a voice. And although I used that confrontational voice in other situations thereafter, it was never in response to the male gaze.

There was no need. Catcalls or once-overs on the street were simply part of the urban scene. And many encounters with the male gaze were welcome, even fun. Half a century later I remember a sudden burst of rain as I was waiting to cross Broadway and a large umbrella opening over me, held by a tall, handsome stranger. We kept an even pace as we walked and talked under that umbrella for two blocks until I reached my destination, and he gave a swift bow and disappeared into the crowd.

I remember other men; occasions when I traveled alone for work or to visit family—less tall or handsome, but interesting, nevertheless. Men who struck up conversations in an airport lounge or hotel lobby or clearly chose the aisle seat when they saw me seated by the window.

It was easy enough to work affectionate mention of my husband into early conversational forays—and though some wandered off, many stayed. A few live on in memory: a constitutional lawyer headed to D.C. to plead at the Supreme Court, a Texas rancher, a filmmaker. We talked until it was time to go, parted with good feeling, and that was that. Each meeting a window into lives different from my own. Each meeting a confirmation of my continued viability. More than viability, agency—the power to attract, to effect action—in the world around me.

By my 50s, I began to notice that the seat next to me remained vacant until occupied by a woman; often, like me, one in her middle years. I colored my hair, let it grow and restyled it into a straighter bob, tweaked my makeup. My dear husband—who always saw me as young and appealing as the day we met—didn't notice. Nor did anyone else.

I had become a hologram, a disembodied mirage. It was to last for 25 years.

Not that long ago, slowly making my way through the heavy revolving door at the Yale Club to attend a memorial service, I felt a shove that practically knocked me over. As the well-dressed shover raced by me, he murmured over his shoulder, "Push!"

And what I had assumed was the male gaze was not gender specific. I would struggle to heave my suitcase onto the overhead rack while the young woman beside me secured her own and took her seat. Even the flight attendant looked right through me as she made her way up the aisle.

Until that day on the bus when—as an object of the geriatric gaze—I was seen again.

It kept on happening. There were "mamas" and even a few "grandmas" from homeless men seated on the sidewalk. When I paused in a store or restaurant to ask directions to the ladies' room (an increasingly common occurrence), people often stopped in their tracks to walk me right up to the door. Hesitating on a curb, wondering whether to charge a heap of snow or attempt a wide stride over a pool of water, someone would wordlessly appear and offer an arm.

It took time to replace "No thanks, I'm okay" with "Thank you very much" to offers of a seat or a helping hand. I now take it as my due. As I move into my ninth decade of life, I have learned that it is at least as blessed to receive as to give—and really rather pleasant.

CONSIDER THE CANE

The cane is the universal symbol of age and frailty. Elderly Crossing signs (a bent woman leaning on a bent man who is leaning on a cane) have appeared on roadways throughout the U.S. and U.K since 1981. Spirited objections, even contests to suggest merrier alternatives, have surfaced from time to time. The signs remain.

Long before there were walkers or wheelchairs, even before the wheel itself, there must have been the cane. It might not appear on the Lascaux cave walls. (The one human figure, reportedly "a bird-headed man with an erect phallus" is not carrying one.) But there were trees—and it's hard to imagine that one of the first hominids to stand upright didn't pick up a limb, lean his weight against it as he walked, and heave a satisfied sigh.

Thousands of years passed. Wood to enamel to plastic. A curved handle and a rubber tip. Holes to adjust to the walker's height. A carrying strap. A folding device. All the colors of the rainbow.

My cane arrived with great hype: "It stands by itself!" Which is true. Unless the floor is uneven. Or there is a carpet. Or a stray waft of air.

I used to need a cane. After the pelvic fractures. Before and after the total hip replacement. The cane transformed me. Taxis summoned with a lunge. Cars—inching up on me as I crossed the street with the light —halted by a wave of my baton. I discovered the power in dependence. Gratefully accepting first dibs on the front seat of the bus or offered a chair while others stood in long ticket lines, I became aware of the power of dependence. Yet I was glad to be rid of the cane; to lose the symbol of disability, to fade into the crowd, a small chip in the "glorious mosaic" of the city.

I manage just fine without a cane. Unless there is ice on the ground. Or snow. Or slippery leaves. Or it is windy. Or it is raining, and the temperature is expected to dip below freezing. Or it is very dark.

I check the weather report. It will be "breezy." When does "breeze" turn into wind? When is wind strong enough to knock a skinny old lady down? I consider the cane.

NECESSARY GIFTS

It was our 30th anniversary and my 80-year-old aunt in Boston surprised us with a gift certificate to a four-star restaurant. It came with instructions. We were to start with martinis, order fish, and not skip dessert. Because I too was raised in Boston at a time when there was only one way to do such things, my thanks were conveyed in a hand-written note on my best notepaper. I opened with "Thank you for a wonderful but totally unnecessary gift."

I went on to describe our menu choices and our pleasure in all, concluding with regret she couldn't be with us and hopes we would all share such a fine dinner together soon. If not a template for Emily Post, I thought it would do.

When I next called my aunt, there was an unusual coldness in her tone. After the obligatory conversation about everyone's health, there was a pause "You are a professor?" She began. "Yes," I answered. Neither she nor I had ever used my academic title. Clearly my book learning had omitted something important, but what?

"I would expect you to know that it is the person who gives the gift who decides what is necessary."

I reacted like a teenager facing an accusing parent, blathering out one excuse after another, each more stupid than the last. The dinner was so generous (she had never been anything but), so unexpected (a major part of the fun) and (worst of all, I cringe to remember it) something we could have done on our own. Eventually I reached, "I was wrong."

Now older than my aunt was then, I look back with new understanding.

I remember that my aunt was ill, soon to die although she kept it secret until the end. I remember how she loved a good time and I never thought to ask why she did not come to celebrate with us. Too late I understand how necessary that gift was to her.

It has been an unusually cold winter. One friend is worn out caring for a sick brother in Canada. I knit her a soft wool scarf that I hope will feel like a hug. Another friend and I exchange idle chatter about hot breakfasts of yore, and I tell her that I have finally found a supermarket that sells Wheatena. "I loved Wheatena," she says. "Haven't seen it in years." I give her a box the next time we meet.

These women had not known Roy, had no memories of us as a couple, never considered me the way I considered myself —a ragged, broken off piece of something that once had been complete. These women, and others who saw me whole, brought me back to life after he died.

They might wonder at my proclivity for small, unexpected offerings. But no one has been so foolish as to call them unnecessary—although of course they are. To everyone but me.

THE STREET BANANA

Early July 1999. I am published in the Metropolitan Diary section of the *New York Times*. They had prepared a whimsical illustration of a woman, banana in one hand, coin in the other, facing a cart of produce and its mustached owner to appear above my entry:

Consider the street banana. Grown in a tropical paradise amid chattering birds and baby monkeys at play, it has traversed thousands of miles over land and sea. On trucks, boats, and trains it has ridden, handled by scores of people, yet its skin is unblemished, its fruit still sweet. You give the man a quarter. He gives you a banana. No change. No receipt. No bag. A transaction direct from the agora. A journey through space and time." Ann Burack-Weiss, New York City

Late November 1999, Roy had a stroke. His body is unimpaired, but no one can say what has happened to his mind. Doctors and therapists have come and gone, asking questions, holding up objects for him to identify. He has said not a word.

I sense he has felt bombarded by people, by sound. I sit silently in the chair beside his bed for a long time and then pull a banana out of my bag and, trying to look casual, take a bite. Then hold it up. "Hey, look what I've got," I say. Slowly he answers, "A banana." Then I say, "But what kind of a banana?" His voice comes out stronger this time. "A street banana."

Roy is still in there. Roy is back. All the way back. He will be back, with me, for ten and a half more years.

THE LAST TIME

Roy often said, "You never know when it's the last time." I don't recall him saying it in reference to a specific kind of event, or, in fact, any event at all. He was given to gnomic observations—and the way they punctuated his everyday speech was one of the things that endeared him to me from our first meeting through over half a century of marriage.

So I doubt he was thinking "last time" on January 2, 2010, as he walked down the driveway of the Montauk house where we had shared 36 years of summers and weekends, where he had built a greenhouse to start summer vegetables from seedlings, where he had built a telescope to look at the stars, where he rolled out the dough for challah on Friday and pasta on Saturday, where we watched the winter sun rise over the ocean, and sat among the treetops on hot summer days.

The plan was to stay over a few days after the holiday week had passed. As always, he had prepared the evening fire after breakfast. Roy built a never-fail fire—crushed newspaper, kindling twigs, and split logs from the dense woods that surrounded us. Then came news of a severe snowstorm on the way, and soon after, the offer of a lift home. We walked down the driveway together without a backward glance. No need. We would be back in a few days.

I returned alone in early April. Roy had died suddenly—but not that surprisingly—in March. We had planned several weekends, but as Friday approached, we found one reason or another not to go. The weather looked forbidding or there was something interesting to do in the city. What we never said to each other, could hardly bear to think ourselves, was that his weak heart was not up to the three-hour trip, let alone close enough to Southampton Hospital. It would not have mattered. But such is the nature of the last time: Plans don't matter.

The house was sold in 2012—the carefully laid fireplace just as Roy had left it.

I am now older than he was when he died, and hardly a day passes when "the last time?" does not flit through my mind. Yet every time we walk down driveway, pick up a book, roast a chicken, watch the spring come again is more than a potential last time. It is also another time (enriched by preceding times) and a first time (something about it will always be new).

I remember that we sat in the back seat of the car, and from the front, were passed a bag of bite-sized peanut butter cups. Neither of us had ever had one. Roy was not one for candy but clearly enjoyed them, and to my amazement, helped himself to a handful.

* * *

I always have a candy dish by the door. It gets most use as guests are leaving, those last few minutes when we hover—saying goodbyes, reviewing the time we just spent, anticipating when we will meet again. Mints are usually there. And chocolate kisses. I watch closely only when someone selects a peanut butter cup. It is not enough to remove the gold outer wrapper; you must also peel off a brown paper frill almost indistinguishable from the gleaming bite within. That it takes a bit of work is as it should be. Not a hard-won pleasure, just one that takes a moment of time and fills it with sweetness.

WIDOW

Her husband had died suddenly. As had mine. It had been a long, close marriage. As was mine. My loss was eight years ago; hers just three months. Perhaps, as someone who had survived a similar loss, I could help?

It was an awkward meeting; we were strangers, linked by a mutual friend. She had a reserve that I sensed was as habitual to her as chattiness was to me. I checked my urge to prattle and listened as she spoke of her husband and the last years they had together. It was easy to see similarities with the life I had with Roy—the semi-retired life of professionals less active than before but still involved in their fields of interest. Each with our own work but sharing the same space for most of every day; pleasure in watching day turn into night, dinner, talk of nothing, talk of everything.

She was clearly expecting words of comfort, if not of wisdom, but what could I tell her?

That those first months felt as if I were living posthumously as if I had died with Roy but somehow part of me was still here. That he had become like the imaginary friend of a child or the phantom limb of an amputee, invisible to everyone but me. And yes, that longing to be pulled into the shadows with him—a sensation I could only fight by acting as if I were still fully of this world; robotic motions of living "normally" tethering me to reality.

After a few months, came a day when the ghost of Roy was no longer at my side. And it got even harder to bear. Our connection had broken, and I was alone. I was a sawed off piece of us making my way through life without the comforting illusion of his presence.

Until around the third, maybe the fourth year (it happened so gradually I can't remember), it changed again. I was no longer the left-over remnant of a couple but a whole person, an entity sufficient to myself. Still alone, still missing Roy but more the idea of Roy; his person no longer quite real to me. Feeling more gratitude for what I had than sorrow for having lost it.

But that took Years! I can't tell her that. At least not now when the wound is so new, so raw; the fight for survival so clear on her face.

Will a bit of levity help? I can't resist the need to bring her back to the here and now.

I look down at her sandaled feet and intone in mock professional certitude, "In my Clinical opinion…you'll be Okay." She looks puzzled. I say, "I see you got yourself a pedicure" She is stunned for a moment, then in all seriousness, asks if I have one too. I kick off my loafers. She gets it! She smiles a weak smile—but it is still a smile—as we look down at twenty bright red toenails ashine in the sun.

THE FACE OF TIME

It is said that by a certain age a woman has the face she deserves. That at about 70 or so, it becomes a map of the person within. I have seen old women like that. Nuns. Vegans. Those whose thoughts were always on higher things. Those for whom a swipe of Chapstick was a beauty routine. You could imagine that they looked like they always had—themselves grown older.

I look like a different being entirely.

Perhaps I overdid the red meat and red wine, baked in the sun before SPF 75, was often less than generous in word or deed. Still, I anticipated a face where glimpses of a younger self could still be seen. I had not imagined wrinkles flowing every which way, eyelids at half-mast, elongated ear lobes, a nose that seems to have grown along Pinocchio lines. A metamorphosis, a shifting and sliding as inevitable as the grooves the receding tide etches on the sand.

I look to the photograph of my great grandfather—Isaac Lander. It is a studio shot circa 1930. He is younger than I am now, a decade past the biblically allotted three score and ten.

Remove the skullcap and replace with a mass of gray curls, shave the beard but for a few random strands undetected in the 10X magnifying glass and there you have me. I look again. He seems to be engaged with someone or something outside the frame. The expression in his eyes is soft, interested, curious. He looks weighed down by the years but still open to life.

Isaac and I never met. All I know of him is that he was born in a small town on the border of Lithuania in 1845 and emigrated to Boston with a wife and five children at the age of 50. I cannot imagine a life so different from my own. Or a face so similar.

Could it be that our old faces may not, in fact, be ones we deserve or even earn? That the vagaries of the lived experience—the choices we make, the good and bad luck that comes our way, even gender differences—take us only so far until the immutable rules of genes, gravity and time take over? That the inner vitality of midlife masked what is now reflected in my mirror?

I wear the face of my tribe. Generations of Jews in Eastern Europe, forced to live apart from the natives of their lands, intermarriages that produced the Semitic features (features mocked in Nazi propaganda films) now replicated in the face in my mirror.

As I carry Isaac's face—our face—from the 19th to the 21st centuries, I am as the flowering plants that cheer the days I spend indoors on cold winter days. I buy them when they are in bud, tend carefully through the height of their beauty, and dispassionately view their withering. They may not bloom again. But somewhere gardeners are preparing new plants from their seeds, mixing them with seeds from other plants, creating something wonderful and new.

CURIOUS

Curious. That word—a word my three-year-old self had never heard attached to anyone else—summed me up in a nutshell. It was not a good thing.

Mine was not a mute curiosity, like sticking a plug into an outlet to test its fit, burrowing into drawers to see what was in there, jumping up on furniture or peering under it to check out the view.

Curious was questions. I didn't ask why the sky was blue or the grass green. I didn't care how the toaster worked. I accepted natural and man-made wonders on their own terms. How they managed to do what they did was none of my business.

Curious was people. On the street, in the butcher store, in the trolley car—a non-stop barrage of questions: Do you have a little girl? Why do you walk so funny? What's in your bag? Where are you going?

Answer me and you were sure to receive follow up questions. What's her name? Will you have an operation? Is it a present? What will you do when you get there?

You couldn't go anywhere with such a child. They managed, in time, to stop me from asking. Then I just stared. I walked right up to where people were sitting, tilted my head way back to get a better look at their faces, peered into their shopping bags, edged in close to listen in on their conversations.

It did not stop until I was about 5. Perhaps reading took its place. Still, "curious" stuck to me as an epithet until I—taking the obvious next step for a curious person from Boston—moved to New York when I was 22.

When I told my mother I had decided to become a social worker, she did not miss a beat. "A perfect job for you —meises (stories) all day long!"

ON THE OTHER HAND

I believe in a woman's right to choose and I believe in the right to life.

I dread end-of-life suffering and I am against assisted suicide.

I believe that hate speech precipitates acts of hate and I believe in the right of everyone to speak and be heard.

I believe in police reform and I believe in law and order.

I try to explain my beliefs about life and death to two beloved millennials and they say, "Grandma, that doesn't make sense!" I try to explain to the same beloved millennials why I believe that speakers known for racist, misogynist, homophobic comments should be allowed to speak on college campuses. They accept that some of my arguments might be sound but protest that logic is not the point—they are talking about Feelings.

Speaking of Feelings....What of the love I hold for America, (country of my birth) and Israel (country of my heart)? What of knowing that the good fortune of my immigrant ancestors was based on stolen land and slave labor and that the Promised Land of the Jews is similarly tarnished?

Yes, I know that no reasonable person thinks in polarities, expresses herself in slogans; that defunding the police means redirecting some of their resources; that one can "love the country and work to eradicate its sin;" and so on down the line.

It is just that I miss the sureness of beliefs that has fled from me through the years. I am obsessively drawn to stories of zealots who switch sides: the Marxist who becomes a Neocon, the White Supremacist who sees the light and devotes his life to advocating for racial justice. Their need for whole-hearted belief, the comfort of allies, is all too clear to me.

I had not a shred of doubt about every war the U.S. has been engaged in since WWII, Civil Rights, Gay Rights, Feminism. I support Roe vs. Wade and am appalled by all efforts to diminish or eradicate it. Silence = Death was not only the sign I marched behind in the AIDS epidemic in the 80s and 90s, it was a core belief

I have kept a bit of certainty. There were not "very fine people on both sides" in Charlottesville, the idea that our country "does not have enough room" for asylum seekers is patently ridiculous.

Then there is this: Only a month ago a woman walked by my bench in Washington Square Park wearing a T-shirt: "Free Abortion on Demand." Flooded with anger, I could barely restrain myself from running after her. Only the facts that I was stunned by the sight (and she was walking Very Fast) held me back.

I support a woman's unalienable rights over her body. But there was such insouciance, such arrogance to the message. As if people who sincerely believe life starts at conception are fit to be scorned. As if all you need to get something is to Demand it. As if anything in life is Free.

Yet, there was a time when I would have worn such a T-shirt with pride, so sure in my rightness, so convinced that any deviation from the script of my group was a sellout.

My response today was surely engendered by advanced age; as well as the sense that polarization has never been so bad, that our country has reached a point where everyone is shouting, no one is listening.

What had started out as a lovely day in the park ended in sadness. And as I slowly made my way home, I wondered: Why do I feel compelled to have an opinion? It's not as if the world is knocking on the door of an 85-year-old woman to find out what she thinks of the events of her day. All I know is that I care now more than I ever have. It seems my debt to the long life I have been given; my responsibility to apply myself to the concerns of those who share this time and place with me, to care about how things turn out for those who will come after me. I can still write the letter, sign the check. But oh, if only there were a group called "On the Other Hand…" to march behind.

THE STAIRS

This loft had stairs! We could come Down the stairs for breakfast in the morning! We could go Up the stairs to bed at night!

We had each grown up in cramped apartments on the outskirts of a major city. Roy's apartment in the shadow of Yankee Stadium in The Bronx where he slept in a kitchen alcove designed to hold a dinette set. Mine in Brighton, Massachusetts where a rarely played baby grand piano—wedged tightly into the cell-sized foyer—forced a sideways slide into the small adjacent rooms.

Growing up in the 1930s and 1940s, neither of us had even been inside a house with stairs. All we knew of them was from outside (windows on top of each other spoke of rooms upon rooms) and from books and movies.

So, although we had since been guests in a variety of two-story houses and knew that stairs could be mounted and descended in misery as well as in joy, to have stairs of one's very own still seemed exotic and wonderful.

Decades passed and we never gave another thought to the stairs. We passed from one floor to another as unthinkingly as we walked room to room on level ground. It never occurred to us to count the stairs (there are 19) or to notice their unusual height or to even touch the banister, a long flat piece of wood that made an attractive wall decoration.

Roy climbed the stairs for the last time on the evening of March 12, 2010. He came down on a stretcher six hours later, borne by two men sent by the funeral home, his body covered by a white cloth.

Stairs began to appear in my dreams. Stairs covered in pale green carpet like ours, stairs of bare wood. Some flights extending endlessly to the sky, others collapsing upon themselves like an accordion.

I began to fall. Bone bruises, pelvic fractures. Assaulted knees and hips responded with arthritic pain. A hip replacement and rehabilitation. Each episode requiring an altered relationship with the stairs.

I began to approach the stairs as a military campaign, standard operating procedures in place with sufficient latitude for unforeseen changes of circumstance.

Things to be carried up or down, placed at debarkation points awaiting the next floor-to-floor maneuver. Empty coffee cups and crumby plates that belong downstairs at the top, just purchased toiletries and books that belong upstairs at the bottom. Sometimes a canvas carrying bag, to sling over my good shoulder lies alongside, sometimes a fanny pack or backpack to free my hands.

I have deliberately slid down the stairs backside first and crawled up on hands and knees. I have walked up one step at a time, intent as a toddler trying out a new skill. I have reached for the banister as for the hand of a caregiver—grasping it a few feet above me to pull up, hang on at hip length to go down.

Then would come a lovely day—sometimes weeks of lovely days—when I could walk up and down almost as easily as I ever did. And it felt again like the time when 19 steps were as nothing, Roy would be waiting for me on the landing, and stairs were still magic.

MONTAUK PERENNIAL

Until I was 35, I only knew two trees—the pine because it had cones; and the oak because of its acorns. I knew a few more flowers: roses, tulips, and orchids that came from the florist, dandelions and daisies that grew in the park.

The house we built in Montauk in 1974 was the first that either Roy or I had ever lived in, and the idea of land took a while to sink in. Our parents, themselves raised in city apartments, were bemused at their first sight of the densely treed acre in Hither Woods: "People actually live here year-round? There are stores somewhere?" Our children, who I imagined delighting in small woodland creatures and collecting specimens for science class, clung terrified to my sides.

Still, we bought. The hilly site had only one plateau, and the builder cleared that spot for a house. The following Sunday we drove out to find a dead deer lying exactly where the foundation was to go. Was this an omen? Would I one day find myself like Elizabeth Taylor in the movie Elephant Walk clinging to a shaky beam as the deer marched single file through the house reclaiming their ancestral home?

Still, we built. Giddy with freedom from street numbers, we named our home for what we were told was our dominant tree, White Oak. We felt like English gentry. All we lacked was a family crest. All I knew of gardens came from English novels. I pictured Dorothea Brooke looking out over that avenue of limes. I pictured Isabel Archer joining the Touchetts and Lord Warburton for tea on the lawn at Gardencourt. Then I looked across our small apron of mossy earth to a dark forest. Perhaps we could add a few things?

We didn't know an azalea from an andromeda, a bulb from a seed. Still, we planted a three-foot-high willow to quench its thirst in the run-off from the outdoor shower. That willow did not weep, it grew. And grew. Swooshing its arms across the roof, shedding leaves on deck and stairs, digging its roots ever deeper into the very underpinnings of the house until we had to cut it down.

Strawberry plants, tulips, crocuses—all became the dining pleasure of rabbits and deer. Exotic blooms suggested for "shade" by growers whose experience clearly did not encompass the Hither Woods drooped and fell.

In 1990, the last of our parents died and the first of our grandchildren was born. White Oak had been spared a takeover by the deer and become an ancestral home for our now grown children who travelled 3,000 miles from each direction to visit each summer. Raking up centuries of leaves, we made a place for wildflowers to take root. And each year put in a few hardy annuals and perennials.

Annuals were graduate students—elements of the group different from one another, clustered together somehow the same—brightly hued, enthusiastic, productive. I tended them carefully, enjoying them when they were there, forgetting them easily when they were not.

Perennials were family, old friends—expected yet full of surprises. I was not a fussy host—staggering their arrival so new ones flowered as old ones faded away, blending individuals in stylish clusters of color and form. I did not keep a log from year to year or chart their locations on graph paper. They bloomed when. they were ready, moved from one spot to another, disappeared, returned. Their subtle colors lingered.

Looking across a still mossy apron of earth, we no longer saw a forest, we saw the trees. The "shad" that bloomed when the shad fish ran died down for a few years but then, inexplicably, came back. The stately beech had a cluster of little descendants around it. The maple and plum we put in did fine. From a forgotten log, green sprouts emerged; the willow tree was planning a comeback.

The trees staged a show twice a year. From October to May, we watched the sun rise over the ocean through their branches. Then they closed the curtain, and we were fanned by a palette of every shade of green. Some, long dead, had become habitats for birds and chipmunks. Our "hurricane tree" (survivor of the legendary storm of 1938) tilted north-northwest, an Olympic training event for generations of squirrels until it gave up the ghost in Hurricane Bob in 1992.

The plants we put in those early years still came up, still were eaten. We were no longer so innocent as to plant them or so foolish as to lament their fate. Deer and rabbits, moles and voles, squirrels, and chipmunks—we all belonged there.

Roy died in 2010 and the house was sold in 2012. Packing up after 40 years, the children and I reminisced about it all—including the dead deer. Every memory of our time there was precious. We worried that the young couple who bought it would tear down the house and rip up the garden as new owners are apt to do. But no, they made changes inside and kept all outside as it was; not even paving the dirt driveway that we cherished among the suburban style bluestone and blacktop driveways that had sprung up all around us.

Last summer, I learned that they were having a baby. What could account for that surge of joy that went through me to hear of this predictable event in the lives of strangers? It just seemed right somehow. Our old life in that house giving way to their new one. Just think.... A baby!

BEING A LADY

It is a mid-week afternoon in 1990. I am waiting in the checkout line with my aunt Ernestine at the Stop & Shop in a middle-class suburb of Boston. It is an established neighborhood of primarily older Jewish residents. A low-income building, housing mostly younger people of color, has recently gone up on the outskirts. My aunt and I are chatting when our attention is drawn to a young Black woman at the register loudly cursing at the cashier, a young white woman who stands cowering in fear.

The customer does not have enough money to cover her purchases.

Freeze frame: The customer blinded with rage at being publicly humiliated. The cashier who looks about to cry. The other shoppers exchanging rolls of the eyes to signal regret for loss of the day when everyone at the market looked like they looked and had enough sense not to fill their carts with items they could not pay for.

My aunt steps out, walks to the head of the line, notes the sum on the register, exchanges a few words with the customer, hands her some cash from her wallet and returns to her place beside me. The customer shrugs, bangs the money on the counter, gathers her groceries and leaves. My aunt does not respond to exclamations from others in line. It is as if she can neither hear nor see them. Nor does she say one word to me. I know better than to speak of it again.

It doesn't matter that the recipient of my aunt's action does not express gratitude any more than it matters what observers see or think. She has an inner compass that guides her behavior through unforeseen situations. It is, simply, what a lady must do: quickly ease over a disturbance in the social order and make as little of it as possible.

One is born a female. One becomes a lady. Table manners began as soon as I was able to hold a knife and fork, broadened into the complexity of Having People Over when I was about six and reached its apotheosis when I was deemed ready for *Etiquette: The Blue Book of Social Usage* at the age of eight.

I listened closely as the ladies of my family debated the cold drink. Do you ask guests if they would like a cold drink (they might want one, but decline, not wanting to put you to the trouble) or just bring out a tray (that might go to waste)? Hospitality required the tray. Then, should you have a selection? Choices might seem the most welcoming; but what of the guest who keeps an eye on the ginger ale as it makes its way around the room only to see it snatched from the tray before it reaches him? To spare him that disappointment, only one drink (lemonade, a general favorite) was best.

Etiquette was one of the four books my parents possessed. It was kept on a low shelf in the china cabinet—a black bible and a gray dictionary standing upright on one side and a large green World Atlas and Gazeteer horizontally positioned on the other.

I loved stories and this book was filled with stories Mrs. Post (born in 1872) was a Victorian lady with a Dickensian sensibility. There was suspense: How would Mrs. Worldly respond to an invitation from Mrs. Nobody? Also, pathos: the fate awaiting Miss Nono Better as painful as the death of Little Nell. Etiquette offered hope. Mastery of the right words and actions was all it took to avoid social catastrophe, to be admired and accepted by all.

I imagined that Mrs. Post's book reflected the adult life I would grow up to lead. A life filled with dances and dinner parties where invitations appeared in one's mailbox and a handwritten response was expected.

It was 1944. With no idea of what girls my age were going through in other parts of the world (the holocaust in Europe, Jim Crow in the United States), I trembled in fear at what might befall me if I failed to write the correct answer and get it in the mail immediately. This last point was essential. One's presumptive hostess could not be kept waiting.

I filled page after page with sample responses, centering them carefully in the model of the original invitation.

> Miss Ann Judith Burack
> Accepts with pleasure
> Your kind invitation....

I waited for the invitations to pour in. Dances and dinner parties did not materialize but—a decade or so later—wedding invitations did. In the 50s, these were all on ivory vellum paper, printed in a script to resemble handwriting. By the time I sent out my own invitations in 1958, response cards and stamped, self-addressed envelopes were in use. My facility at a written response to a happy or sad occasion was translated to carefully composed messages on monogrammed note paper.

Through the years my standards lessened but never left. The phone call often replaced the note, museum cards instead of monogrammed note paper,. Hallmark remained beyond the pale.

* * * *

It is a summer afternoon in 2020. I am invited to a small gathering in Montauk. The host introduces me to his mother-in-law just in from Minneapolis. The murder of George Floyd fresh on my mind, I make a comment about the tragedy of the event. To which she responds, "It's a wonderful city. I don't know why they're making such a big fuss over it." I sit silently and the conversation moves on.

Why did I not speak out? Women I admire dare to forego company manners, risk disapproval by challenging the opinions of others and here I am trying to keep everyone (including myself) comfortable. While I sign petitions, march in protests, and donate money to support social justice, I cave in when standing alone. Ensuring that no one will be disappointed by the cold drink too often on my mind.

Can I say, as Aunt Ernestine would, "It was not the time or the place?" The words of Rabbi Hillel rise up to silence me. "If I am not for myself, who will be for me? But if I am only for myself, what am I? If not now, when?"

Every argument for authenticity but this: My authentic self is not all that wonderful. If there is anything I like better than hearing a juicy piece of gossip, it is spreading it around. I am opinionated, impulsive, impatient. It is in my nature to be the first to speak, to push to the head of the line. If I didn't have guardrails to restrain me, the opinions of others would not matter. I would not think well of myself.

I am consoled when I remember the first rhyme I was ever taught: "A lady will always do and say/the kindest thing in the nicest way." If not the finest creed to aspire to, it is not the worst.

IT'S IN THE BAG

Many years ago, I volunteered at a homeless shelter for women over 45 collectively and universally known as "the ladies"), housed in a mixed-use building on Park Avenue—the center of the toniest area of New York City. I was teaching in a graduate social work program and came at the suggestion of an employee, a former student who thought that I—a gerontologist specializing in narrative and women's issues—might find it "interesting."

The staff jointly decided that I should lead a Story Group. "Tell a Story, Hear a Story, Stories with Ann" was placed on the weekly schedule for Tuesday afternoons at 3:00 pm. The assigned room was small, previously unused, far from the hub of the shelter. I knew that the chances of attracting and holding a group was slim. I needed a draw. Food was my default.

The group began for me at noon where I searched out items in supermarket aisles that would be sufficiently enticing to coax the ladies over the threshold as well as meet stringent requirements. It was a varied selection, soft for those without teeth, pre-wrapped for easy slipping into a waiting pocket.

By 1:00 pm, I was at the shelter—food stowed —walking around and talking to whoever would talk to me. The 80 residents were so diverse as to defy easy categorization. They were alike only in lacking permanent housing—a fact of greater urgency to the staff than to them.

Over half were born and grew up in other parts of the country, other parts of the world. Little in the way of "psycho-social history" made its way into client records. The ladies were under no requirement to provide it and rarely volunteered. They themselves made the most crucial delineation: those who "had the voices" and those who didn't.

Those who "had the voices" (auditory hallucinations associated with schizophrenia) were seen as privileged by those who didn't. They were more likely to be white, their manner hinted at a fall from higher status, and they received professional attention—doctor visits and medications seen as desirable. The others were more likely to be women of color whose demeanor suggested a life of hard times.

The dormitories were closed for most of the day. Some of the ladies chose to spend that time inside and some chose to roam. My only impression of the roamers I passed on the elevator each Tuesday were that many of them looked better going out than I looked going in. Tastefully dressed, carefully made-up, temporarily unencumbered by their possessions—they had the "put together" look that matched the Zip Code.

My work was with the women who remained. Some walked aimlessly around the huge entry space. Some sat on the hard chairs randomly scattered about, eyes focused on some middle distance. A few ladies were always congregated about the laundry room loudly arguing a familiar communal issue: Do you have the right to remove clothes from the dryer if the owner doesn't appear when the cycle is done?

Few were interested in hearing about the group. One of the women who "had the voices" found out that I came from Columbia University and wanted to know if I had studied Psychology. I had barely nodded when she asked what I thought of Freud: Would he change his opinion about women if he lived today? We agreed that he probably would and had a 10-minute discussion that would not have been out of place in a seminar room. The next week she began shouting the moment I came into view. "Why do you want me to get married? Why don't you just leave me alone?" She steered clear of me ever after,

Even with the lure of interesting snacks, the idea of coming to a Story Group was hard to sell. Program material was needed. The ladies who were not up to sitting around a table and talking could relate to each other around a common activity.

Most successful were things they got to keep when the meeting was over. One afternoon I brought in a collection of perfume testers from Bloomingdales. For a brief time, we were simply a group of older ladies inhaling new scents and recalling the iconic ones of the 50s and 60s, the mystique and packaging of "Taboo," and, as one woman put it, "the summer everyone wore 'Charley'."

One Tuesday, after a storm had left the shoreline near my Montauk house strewn with treasures, I brought in an assortment: beach glass, scallop shells, small white stones, golden dingles with holes seemingly made for stringing, beach glass, starfish—even seaweed and sand. Some of the women recalled happier days on the sugar sands of Antigua, the oatmeal sands of Coney Island, the contrasting sands of Montserrat—pink on one beach, black from volcanic ash on another. Only a few were interested in taking an item. All coveted the varied bags in which the collection was packed. Even those hat smelled of the sea were acceptable. Rinsed and dried they would be good as new.

By then I knew about the importance of bags. I had been upstairs to the dormitory where eight rows of beds—ten to a row—were lined up with a narrow passageway between them. From 8-3:00, when the floor was cleared for mopping, each bed was piled with the possessions of its occupant.

Most of the ladies had lots of stuff they were constantly sifting through. Without the organizational aid of closets, cabinets, shelves, and drawers, extricating an object and replacing it takes lots of time. Papers and fabrics must be unfolded and refolded. Bungee cords or tape unfastened and re-fastened.

A few had found beat-up suitcases to fit everything in; most relied on large black plastic bags of the type that burly men in commercials use to hurl unwanted debris to the curbside for disposal—trash bags.

Each bag was a personal statement. Jody always came to group bedecked: many rings; several on each ear, up to the knuckle on each finger. About her neck and wrists, hung other ornaments. She was as eager to show me the contents of her bag as I was to see it. Small boxes, and stained remnants of silk and satin lingerie contained more rings, bracelets, necklaces, and shiny objects (chains, buttons, beads) that looked like they could be jewelry if they tried harder. You'd know her bag anywhere

The homeless men I saw on the streets were rarely encumbered. When they did tote bags, the black plastic bulged with the hard edges of tradeable sundries—redeemable soda bottles or found objects to array for sale on a sidewalk blanket. The ladies in contrast, had soft, squashable bags—a layer of insulation between them and the world.

I made my decision on the spot. I would collect bags. More than enough bags for everyone. After all, bags—like the best things in life—are free. Bags of paper and plastic, all sizes. The prettiest bags from the swankiest stores. Hopeful symbols would replace damning ones. For those moving on to permanent housing—Bed, Bath & Beyond. For those in recovery, working to put first things first—ABC Carpet & Home. For those with romance on the mind—Today's Man and Victoria's Secret. If large, strong bags were a necessity, small fancy bags would add a touch of luxury. Mightn't bag karma follow?

A middle-class woman of a certain age can amass many bags in a short amount of time. Cashiers at department and home furnishing stores, purveyors of the largest bags, slipped in a few extras at my request. The smallest bags, previously scorned in the name of environmentalism, were now ardently pursued. I entered stores I had only walked past before, bags on my mind.

Lip gloss from Henri Bendel, sun block from Bergdorf's—prices close to the same everywhere, but only here the uselessly elegant bags with string handles made to dangle on the arms of ladies who lunch.

Amazed I surveyed the haul—a mountain of bags in a matter of weeks. I had not gone on a shopping spree. In fact, it was hard to recall any of the items I had carted home in them. Muffin tins and coat hangers, pantyhose and pillowcases, unthinking everyday purchases. It was only then that I realized the obvious. Bags are not free. Bags go to those who buy what they need not those who beg or find it.

I continued—the collection stored in (yes) large plastic trash bags in the back of the hall closet. Like the ladies, I would often take them out and sort through. When there seemed to be enough, I decided to tell staff about the bags and find out what day would be best to bring them in.

The director shuddered. Her assistant groaned. John, the former student, patiently explained: Any bags the ladies received would immediately be filled. In the interest of safety, sanitation, and sanity they spent hours each week trying to get rid of stuff, not add to it. There was no way they could accept the bags.

The Recycling Center in Montauk is a model of organization. Plastic here. Paper there. Again, I rifled through and categorized. And there left all the bags.

Soon I left the shelter as well. My memory balks at the reason why. I remember it was because the time slot and room assigned to me was preempted by a consultant psychiatrist. But then, I might have rescheduled, if I had really wanted to? And I never promised to stay more than a semester, did I? Like the ladies, I sift and rearrange the reasons and pad them softly so I can carry them around.

REVERSE ALCHEMY

1989   GMHC (Gay Men's Health Crisis)
Think Sharon Stone. Think again. The jeans and tee shirt have been washed too often. She is clean but not polished - model thin, as blondely and blandly gorgeous as a statue at Madame Tussaud's. Her eyes and bearing give nothing away. In her arms is a smiley baby, squirmy as she is still, black as she is fair. The baby is not hers. Its mother is in prison. How did she get it from the clutches of the child welfare system? The story so unbelievable, it has to be true. Why did she want it? "Every lonely girl wants a baby." Now she is seeking a legal adoption. She has been on methadone maintenance for a year now and has full blown AIDS, the baby was born HIV+ with a good chance of being rid of the virus after a year. For this reason, she has named the baby Hope.

The 12-page intake form lies on the gray Formica cube between the color coordinated loveseat and chairs in this not-living room where noise from the air-filter machine forces us to shout the unspeakable. I have been doing this for twenty years.   I work in New York City at not-for-profit social agencies set up to help adults—the chronically ill, the disabled, and those who are, simply, old and alone. Unlike welfare departments that provide money, the agencies I work for provide services. Services are predominantly verbs turned nouns (placement in protective care) and nouns turned verbs ("transitioning" from hospital to home). Services don't give people what they want but help them live with what they get.

My title is "social worker." My task today is "intake." This morning I will be a reverse alchemist; converting the gold of story into the dross of data, the life into the case history, the case history into the file. I am, as the expression goes, "good at what I do."

Like an investigative reporter, I stop at nothing to get the story.   I go to them. To home visits where I sit on the hard chair—drinking, from questionable cups, the coffee offered me.   To hospitals in that hour after visitors leave when it is always Fitzgerald's 3:00 am of the soul. To "congregate" settings where specially outfitted vans have delivered the solitary to socialization in the early-afternoon lull after lunch and before cards. To the hallways of those municipal buildings that traffic in human misery. Usually, they come to me. To offices that look like rabbit warrens and offices that look like offices and offices like this, the saddest kind, that try to look like home. Surroundings matter less than you would think.

When I started doing this, all the people I loved were still alive. I had not yet sat on the other side of the desk or lain in the hospital bed or awakened at exactly 6:00 am to a ringing phone and known, in that instant before picking up the receiver, the sureness of disaster. I had no idea how many ways there were for life to have its way with you.

I hold power. It took me a long time to sit comfortably with that. Longer still to sit uncomfortably. In the early years, I pushed my desk against the wall so that my chair and the one in which the client sat faced each other without a barrier in between—as if equality in the seating arrangement could erase the fact that I was white and well off when they were black and poor, that I was young and healthy when they were old and sick, that they were asking me for something that meant the world to them and I could refuse as readily as not. I sit uncomfortably now, but strangely at ease. I do what I can. As do they.

My interview style, formulated when there was world enough and time, has fallen out of favor in the profession. I am now expected to read all questions from the intake form — cunningly designed to move from the innocuous to the intrusive —and record the answers as we speak. Because I am confident that all that I need to know will emerge in the course of our talk, I will fill in most of the spaces later. There are always numbers to be filled in and documenting papers to be collected. I have turned down the corner of pages that require signature (release for information and agency contract) and identification numbers (Social Security, public assistance, Medicaid) and names (personal and professional "supports") to be completed before the applicant leaves. Between then (an hour and a half away) and now there is the lonely girl, the happy baby and me in a soundproof windowless room.

I admire the baby's large eyes and long lashes and without a word The Lonely Girl hands her to me. Hope knows both games in my repertoire: Where's the baby, this little piggy, and greets each with shrieks of delight. "You must play with her a lot," I say. "Such a social baby for a quiet mother," I think. "What could this story be?" Except for the busy clinic doctors, no one other than The Lonely Girl held Hope until I did. The ice breaks. The story pours out. Once started talking it is hard for her to stop. Problems for which there are no remedies in our arsenal. Wishes deferred, adjourned, forgotten. ignored, for so long that they formed the crater in which Hope cuddles and thrives.

Some stories come out like hers, in fits and starts; the inner voice a few words ahead of what I hear. These are the virgin stories —simultaneous translations, revealing themselves to the speaker as they do to me. They are rare because most applicants have told their stories to social workers many times and have obligingly perfected set pieces tailored to fit the spaces on the ubiquitous form.

Applicants often lie. Lies are the currency of the powerless. Of trading value with the outside, they are even more valuable to the self. Lies link together the weak pieces of home and relationship, putty in the empty space of work and meaning. In the telling, would, could, and should become did, do and will. The stories roll on. I don't challenge. They tell lies but speak the truth. I listen.

I nod a lot. And sometimes murmur "yes" or "uh huh". I notice when words and eyes don't agree. I ask for specifics. If the family is "dysfunctional" I ask in what way. When I hear that a stepfather is "abusive" I ask to hear an example; I am sorry when I do.

The Lonely Girl knows what she wants. She wants to be well and have legal custody of Hope. Legal custody is not granted to solitary women on methadone with life threatening illnesses. So, I too am involved in simultaneous translation from what she wants to the services available on the referral list. She mentions the weak lock on her door at the welfare hotel, the shooting last week at the bodega down the block not two minutes after she left, and I think "housing." She adds that she had just bought a package of cheese doodles and a coke for dinner, and I think "nutritional counseling" and "meals program". She tells of the boyfriend who died only last month and the family who wants no part of her, and I wonder, "bereavement group" or "support group?" She has needs that could keep ten agencies busy for ten years - if she has that long. And if she doesn't - the wound she does not look at, the scar that will rip open perhaps before it is torn - what will happen to Hope if (when?) something happens to her? I want to tell The Lonely Girl that everything will work out for her. I want to hand over all the cash in my wallet. I want to take them home with me. I don't. We first shake hands and then, awkwardly, hug. Hope waves bye bye. We will not meet again.

Alone with the form, my reverse alchemy begins. Converting a life into a case is delicate work. Carving my way around the pain of The Lonely Girl's life like a surgeon avoiding the bloodletting artery, I deconstruct the information she gave me refashioning it into hard beads of information known as Data. I place an X in the appropriate check-off places and fill the blank lines with short phrases. The last section of the page is left for my Assessment and Plan. Here, I must force the data into a pattern; a cause-and-effect scenario that will justify the agency's provision of services and specifies what those services will be. The words of old teachers guide me. Each step is a building block to the next. Each service in the Plan must relate to a problem in the Assessment. Each problem in the Assessment must relate to facts in the Data. The Lonely Girl's story fits the data as the feet of Cinderella's stepsisters fit into the glass slipper. The old teachers did not say what to do with the leftovers—the facts that explain nothing, the Assessment for which only God has a Plan. Maybe.

A small space is left for Impressions. How can I describe this particular mother and child? Perhaps some time with the Bible or Shakespeare would yield a phrase to capture her beauty, her strength, her doom. Such literacy is neither required nor desired. Shorthand suffices: High Risk. ASAP. That about does it.

All done but the papers - I turn to the wad she pulled out of her worn pink diaper bag. Papers are data digested and regurgitated from files in other agencies. Some papers are folded the size of postage stamps, smelling of the pocket and the purse. Others are barely readable bleached out copies of copies. Or time-worn, darkened, and splitting at the creases. In these papers, professionals who have filled out and receive them communicate over the heads of the people whose fate they hold - like parents spelling out what they don't want the children to hear

Seasoned applicants have their papers together. Some have found a clip. They usually ask for more copies (to sell? to insure against future loss?) It's my call. Those who are new to the system may hand over their only copy, unaware of its value, of what it will take to get a replacement. (I shudder at such carelessness. "Here, take these copies. You'll need them"). Those who present a manila folder with flat papers are usually not applicants themselves but seeking help for incapacitated others. This is not about me, the unruffled papers say. If the well-ordered papers are presented by applicants, they are as totems carried into an unfamiliar world - a begging attempt at equality. I understand your need, they say. I once had a job about papers myself.

I staple the papers to the intake form and stuff it all into a manila envelope. I scrawl a large" confidential" across the envelope before dropping it into the slot of a domed metal container, shaped like a breadbox, constructed for the purpose. And suddenly flash on a valentine box on the desk of a third grade teacher in that brief moment after the hopes go in, before the truth comes out.

2021

I rarely venture outside of my orbit now but there were many years when I attended social gatherings of strangers where "what do you do?" was an introductory gambit.

I recall a few such moments. The dinner party where the gentleman at my right said, "venture capitalist" and I said, "social worker." We were so far out of any common ground that we sat in stunned silence.

My favorite responses to hearing that I was a social worker: "How gutsy of you!" and "I could never do that, I feel things too much."

The most common reaction was "Isn't it depressing? I would try to explain: "Humbling, Privileged, Inspiring." True words that rang false as soon as they hit the air. Then I stopped trying, just said "no" and changed the subject

What I still cannot explain, even to myself, is how all the people I met abide within me.

I have entered hundreds of lives, looked around, and left. A dozen or so, like The Lonely Girl, remain as clear in my mind's eye as the day we met. Of the others, I remember few faces, fewer names.   Just a feeling remains. Or the fragment of a dream that I recognize on awakening comes from someone else's life.

Unmoored from their moment, remembered stories rise and fall within me like the tide: cautionary tales, how-to guides, homilies, pained comedies, ironic tragedies. They have expanded the one life I have been given into a universe of lives, a universe of lessons on living.

THE PERSISTENCE
OF MEMORY

Dali's inspiration for "The Persistence of Memory"—his iconic painting of limp watches —was the sight of a Camembert cheese melting in the sun. Rushing to a landscape in process (rocky cliff, barren tree, sea), he picked up a brush. He did not paint cheese. He painted time.

Actual time melting. Remembered time spreading. Nothing looks like it should look, is where it should be, does what it should do. Hang on tight, it won't stop the slide down the well of time.

Dali was supposedly inspired by the great thinkers of his day: Einstein's theory of relativity, Freud's theory of dreams and the unconscious. I cannot look at "The Persistence of Memory" without thinking of dementia.

Back in the 1960s, "dementia" was not part of the professional lexicon. It was a lay word used in a derogatory way to describe someone who did or said something a bit strange. ("That sounds like something Charley would do. He's demented!")

OMS (Organic Mental Syndrome) or OBS (Organic Brain Syndrome) frequently appeared at the head of the list of an older person's diagnoses. Handwritten—as medical charts were in those days—the capital letters took up more space than the lowercase ailments that followed; messaging it as the most important thing to know about the patient.

"Hardening of the arteries in the head" was the explanation. Alzheimer's disease was reserved for early onset cases and there was virtually no recognition of other diseases, vascular changes, or reversible states (the shock of hospitalization, over-medication) that could present in a similar way.

As the years passed and the knowledge base grew, I kept up. I learned about the neurology, the psychology, the social impact. I met with husbands, wives, adult children, and grandchildren as they poured out the pain of seeing the person who meant the world to them change before their eyes. I sat with their loved ones, doing my best to connect with the spark that sometimes appeared in their eyes, their movements.

Yet, even as I practiced, read, and taught about dementia, it always felt outside the clinical realm. I thought of it as exile to a foreign country. And remembered that country back in the 1970s on the 5th floor of the long-term facility where I worked. You stepped off the elevator into a dreamscape. Old women lost in time. Some slumped in wheelchairs. Others pacing the halls. One crying, "Mama." Another tearing off her clothes.

You can know the customs of a people, you can study their daily practices, you can pore over their artifacts, only when you communicate in their language, can you try to enter the life.

Late-stage dementia has no native speakers. One could call it an acquired tongue, but for its indeterminacy, the sparseness of words. All in the present tense, no rules of grammar, no written form. To understand it requires attention to sighs, moans, groans, shifts in the expression of the eyes, loosing and tightening of the skin around the mouth, gestures of the hands and feet, movements of the torso.

To speak it is to enter the world of limp watches on dried wood as a respectful guest, accepting cues on your behavior from a host who has no idea why you are there.

It begins before you enter the room. Slowing your body, mind, voice, pace. Then you sit close, at eye level, connecting your being with the one before you. Giving time to get used to the idea of you being there for them: your name, the names from the person's past that might ring that far off bell ("your handsome grandson Scott"). Looking for the slightest flicker of the eye at that.

Speaking dementia is to abandon the R word: "Remember." If not as obviously offensive as the N word posing a memory test to someone who is likely to fail is no less demeaning. It is also to choke back the W words (Who, What, Where, When, Why) that crowd your larynx shouting to be let out. A question expecting an answer is a blunt affront to the mores of the country.

To speak dementia is, very often, to be silent.

The man moans and you may say "it is hard." Or just nod. Maybe pat a hand or his back. The woman reaches out to the beads around your neck—say "pretty" or just sit there holding them. And you may hold it up for a closer look, perhaps note that her hair was just set, "curly, nice." Smiles, a few words, touch—a bridge connecting two people celebrating their both being alive in the universe, in the same space, at the same time.

* * *

As people remember where they were on 9/11, I remember where I was when I first heard the statistics. It was 1987. A large meeting of gerontoloists on another topic. We were just getting settled when someone mentioned n article that had appeared on the front page that morning announcing the ncreasing likelihood of dementia after the age of 65. The numbers were jaw ropping—especially for those over 85 when the odds were 1 in 3. Two re-earchers refuted the data. It had been around for a while, they said, and the nethods were questionable: sloppy sampling, questions about the coding. uture studies would surely prove them wrong.

Thirty-five years have passed. Later studies have proved the initial findings vrong. The odds of developing dementia over 85 are now believed to be 1 n 2.

Two old friends have already slipped across the border to the country of ementia. I am tempted to write that it is ironic since they were both geron-ological social workers who worked alongside me. One was a gifted clini-ian and administrator; the other a writer and trainer whose words moved nany to take up the work. It is not ironic. O'Henry is ironic. It is probability.

Each has taken a bit of me into that Dali dreamscape where the pieces of ur friendship lie scattered on the sand. The me that talked about books with ne, politics with the other. They have passed beyond books and politics. Because of distance, we now communicate by phone.

C. still has words and is noting her decline clinically. "Mild to moderate," he informs me from the memory care unit where she has recently moved. he still has a sense of time and place. Our talk will be brief, she says, as she ; due for a meeting where they read poems and imagine who wrote them, vho they were written to. (I wonder at this as a memory exercise. Could it e she has it wrong? Or is moving into the world of imagination a new way f connecting with dementia patients?) How I would like to discuss with my ormer colleague—but she is no longer there.

J. is further along. She still has her trademark giggle, but her speech is halt-ng, drifts off mid-sentence. She will see me soon, sometime, tomorrow, next veek? We will get together when she gets back home, she is away now, in this place. It is not a bad place, but she wants to get home. (She is, of course, at ome. Her husband answered the phone and quickly handed it over. I picture im there seated beside her. How long can they go on like this?)

I speak to C. and J. as I learned (with them, from them) long ago. Good mes from the past with strong descriptive words that I hope will reach cross miles of airways, masses of plaques and tangles, to reach the self I new and loved.

How I long to use the R word that holds our pasts. The W words that vould let me into their heads

I want to order a new baking dish and sit down at the computer. I start to write Cuisinart but even before I finish typing the word, I realize it is not right. I do not want a food processor. What I want is...I play charades with myself. Starts with C. Two syllables. Sounds like....C...C. It is a.... Yes Creuset. That is it. Triumphant but shaking, I type the word and a comforting array of just the dishes I want appears before me.

I am sharpening my tacks. I am hanging on to my marbles.

Count backward from 100 by 7s? I've got it covered.

Animals? Fruits? Flowers? No problem.

Jobs that begin with a letter. Dynamite with As and Bs. Working on my Ls Lawyer, Linguist, Lithographer. How many do I need in how many minutes?

How are apples and oranges alike? Answer "they are fruit" and you are okay. Answer "they are round" and you are heading into Dali Territory. I must not forget. It is never about the thing—always the category. How will I think then? When? Maybe it will be as something you don't see in front of you but a big box in which the thing belongs. But what if I don't remember the words, where they keep the box, what they call it?

I am building a sandcastle on the beach, securing the moat with wet sand packed tight. The water flows in slowly at first, a calm trickle, a little swimming pool. Then the big wave. The walls shatter first, then the castle. The wave, unknowing and uncaring, recedes. Was the castle ever there?

The Persistence of Memory hangs in the Museum of Modern Art. It is small—the size of a piece of notebook paper. I read all about it. Dali's fascination with the world of dreams. The petrified piece of wood his self-portrait.

I look and read. Read and look. The terror remains.

SOMETIMES I FORGET

Sometimes I forget. Especially when the weather takes a turn toward chill, and the store windows are filled with fall fashions. I see a well-cut plaid skirt in beige and black, note it would look smashing with a turtleneck in either color, and think, "Just what I need."

I imagine that I will leave the shop with both the skirt and a beautiful, beaded sweater that caught my eye. That although there is no gala occasion to wear the sweater coming up, there is sure to be one before long. And won't I be pleased with myself for having thought ahead!

Sometimes I forget. Especially on a crisp October day like today. I imagine that I will get up tomorrow morning and decide what clothes best suit where I'm headed. A teaching day? A library day? Field visits to social agencies? Lunch with colleagues? Department meetings? A play or concert in the evening? That I'll ponder the chance of rain before tugging on suede boots—taking my chances because they go so well with what I have on.

That I will brush out my long hair—pulled back straight from my forehead—before settling on chignon, French braid, or round bun. That V-neck sweaters worn with large hoop earrings (silver one day, gold the next) still look good on me.

So easy it is to forget—on this day that shouts "back to work"—that the life I once had, the body I once dressed for that life, is no longer mine.

So hard to remember that a changed hairline dictates a curly, no-nonsense bob. That a shorter shape and diminishing waistline precludes many clothing choices and a reduced round of outside activities takes care of the rest. That yoga outfits, black pants, black skirt, and a few tops, are all the clothes I will need for the rest of my life.

Sometimes, I just forget.

ON THE BEACH

In the Boston of the 1940s, those confined to their homes were known as "shut-ins" and advice to "remember" them poured out of the radio every holiday. I could not forget even on ordinary days. My walk to school passed by a ground floor window where one of them sat—a girl of about my age, her back so strangely twisted that her chin appeared to be resting on her shoulder. Noticing her noticing me, I would force a cheery smile. She stared back.

She was always fussing with the costume of one or another of an enormous collection of Storybook dolls and would lift it up to show me. Whether she was taunting me with ownership or telling me that shut-in life was not so bad, I was never to find out. She was less and less at the window, until one day I realized she was gone for good.

Looking through that window, I could not have imagined that entering the world of shut-ins would become my life's work.

I've spent countless hours in the company of people whose landscape is bounded by bed, chair, and bathroom. They moved from one to the other with difficulty—leaning on canes, walkers, and available arms—landing heavily with sighs of relief. There were a few for whom bodily confinement allowed the spirit to expand. Most shrank, their essence becoming smaller and meaner than the rooms they occupied.

I have been peering into vacant eyes forever, trying to understand what is going on in there. What exactly is missing. Reason? Memory? Hope? In those eyes I have seen glints of terror and flashes of anger and sadness so black and deep that it hurts to look. I have seen eyes filled with birthday candle lights atop frail bodies that still move in tune to the music and rejoice in the gleeful gluttony of soft cold ice cream.

In an agency for the blind where numbered beeps announced the floors, I learned to describe things I realized I had never really looked at before. I learned that fingers could read. In an agency for the deaf, eerie quiet was broken only by coughs and, shockingly raucous laughter. I learned to tap people on the shoulder when I wanted their attention. I learned that fingers could speak.

I now know how they do it. Could I?

* * *

It is early Monday morning, and the deserted Montauk beach is teeming with action. The sun beats down from the east. The waves are oversized, haphazard, wildly crashing at three different places on the horizon. Although there is only a light breeze and a few wispy clouds, I know that this evening's news will report a storm heading our way. The incoming tide is almost to the high-water mark, chiseling out large scallops of dark sand on light—designer shades of taupe and ecru. Seagulls have congregated around a spot in the ocean where a school of fish must be passing.

I consider: What if I couldn't get down here on my own? Yes. Being here would be enough even if (and I blanch here) I'm not fully aware of where I am. Knowing or even caring about the ways of storms and seagulls is not essential to the scene. In the drift of an unmoored mind, I could give myself up to the play of light on the waves, the satisfying whoosh and bang as they break.

Without sight? I close my eyes. The beach sounds arrange themselves into a modern musical composition. Cacophony. Silence. A cymbal wave. A loud bird that must be near. A softer bird (smaller or further away?) a Xylophone wave, a lack of pattern, a pattern.

On an impulse, I dig into my pockets and come up with a wad of tissue. I fashion earplugs and insert them. Eyes open, the scene becomes a moving painting in which I notice, the interplay of horizontal and vertical. The sand-pipers to the far left, the herring gulls in the near right, united by the patch of white—a color accented by the cloud overhead.

I am suddenly aware that the sand under me is cold, and the cold is working itself up into me. I pick up a handful of sand and sift it through my hands. There are many textures in one handful—a smooth hard big clump, loose and soft trickles.

I notice a smell. Not the pungent salt of the New England beaches of my youth but a lighter, more variegated brew in which only the scent of seaweed is identifiable. I lick my arm. Does it taste like spinach or is it only my association? The sun on my feet feels warmly personal, as if it has chosen to shine only on me.

Enough. I open my eyes, remove the earplugs. The scene is so bright, so oud—an overwhelming embarrassment of riches.

I can no longer coil and leap from the sand. No one is here to observe my graceless, bolstered on one arm, ascent. Once upright, I walk across the beach and up the dune. My pace through the heavy sand is sort of a slow shuffle, bending slightly forward to hold my balance. I stop at the top for one last look.

Why am I being so dramatic? I have been coming to this beach for decades and expect to do so again, but life offers no promises. This morning might be the last. I must remember it.

IN THE VORTEX

I am 10 years old. The first night home after my tonsils come out, I begin to cough. Scabs and blood fill the yellow enamel pail with the green rim. Doctor and ambulance follow. My nose is packed with cotton. Sirens scream. Outside the hospital are bright lights; nurses wearing big white hats hold out their arms to me. I am flat on a table, more bright lights. I want to sleep but they keep slapping me awake, calling my name. The next thing I remember must have been a day or two later. I am in bed and two young nurses enter, they carry scissors and speak in a soft Irish brogue. My hair is matted with dried blood. They must cut it all off.

I am a tall, skinny girl with a curved back. "What beautiful hair!" is the only compliment on my looks I have ever received. My hair is long, thick, dark and carries a miraculous wave. With it you can shape corkscrew curls that rival those of Shirley Temple.

"You cannot cut my hair!" I cry. Perhaps they take pity on me or fear that I will begin to cough again; but they soon agree. They leave and return with a bottle of oil and thick toothed combs. It is long, rough going. The oil needs time to soak in, it hurts as the comb is dragged through. The washing reveals missed areas—back to the oil, the combs, the washing. Finally, they are done.

I am handed a mirror. It is hard to take in who I am looking at. This chalk-white face cannot be me. But, of course, it is. When they leave, I go to sit by the window.

I am in the Floating Hospital for Children in Boston—recently re-established on land—and the window faces a deserted block by the harbor. I look out at the dilapidated buildings (as clear in my mind's eye today as the view I see each day from my bedroom window). And I say to myself in an adult voice that I don't recognize "You were going to die, now you are going to live."

* * *

I am seated in a small room, conducting an intake interview. I face a young woman who is telling me about her descent into crack addiction and the day she decided she had to quit. It is a harrowing story. I am listening hard. She has just said that she looked in the mirror and couldn't recognize herself. I am there with her.

Then .... I feel us rising from our chairs, swept up and swirling in a vortex. I am no longer a social worker. She is no longer a client. Our identities have been stripped away. We are pure spirits—disembodied beings passing each other in the same swirling pattern, tiny molecules up there in space.

Then...we are back in the office, returned to ourselves. She is still speaking of the mirror. How much time could have passed—not as long as a minute, seconds, perhaps?

One transcendent experience in a long life does not a mystic make. And it is possible that the image of an unfamiliar face in a mirror performed some neurological voodoo. Yet, whenever I think of the hereafter, I picture myself and my beloved dead as spirits whirling around in the vortex. The vortex contains all the souls who ever lived—those blessed with the riches of life, those who had the hardest of fates, those who died at birth, those who lived on to a ripe old age—all now equal parts of the same whole—awhirl, awhirl in the universe

ROLE OF A LIFETIME

I've received compliments in my day. Something I'd cooked, written, said. a new hair style or dress. Not so many that I took them for granted. Not so few that I felt deprived. Just the amount one would expect for a woman of my appearance and abilities. So, it was a surprise when—around the time I turned 80—I began receiving accolades for nothing more than being me; kept being told that I was "amazing" and "an inspiration."

At first, I chalked it up to surprise that someone of my years could actually function as a "normal" (i.e., mid-life) person. Recently though, I've begun to wonder if, indeed, Old Woman was the role in life I was born to play.

Some women do best in late adolescence and early adulthood—the peak of sexual desire and desirability. Others bloom in family life—their finest hours devoted to children and home. Still others recall their work lives as the time they came into their own. Happy memories of these times of life gladden my heart but are recalled as a blur. Flash photography. Here I am doing this. Here I am doing that...

It was not that I didn't enjoy most of it or do some things well; just that there was never a breakout performance, a time when I could not have done better. I don't know if it was the plots or the scripts or the other actors, but I experienced much of my life as a succession of challenges that kept me breathless—hit or miss performances by someone who barely mastered one set of lines before being handed another.

The plots were often too complicated to follow, starting out simply and opening up to complications and changes that left me struggling to keep up. Fellow actors were a rapidly changing cast: my children as they passed through various ages and stages, students who came and went, colleagues who changed with every venture, clients who needed more than I could give, friends going through all manner of jobs and relationships. My husband a co-star in many productions, absent in some. Constantly adjusting, compromising, calibrating my responses to those who shared the stage with me.

And the sets. So many rooms—each requiring a different costume, script skills. I was a lover in the bedroom, a chef in the kitchen, a hostess in the living room, a teacher in the classroom, a therapist in the consulting room and a mother (Where are the children? Are they okay?) everywhere, always.

Was this life foisted upon me? Was I dragged to the theatre and forced to perform by a rigid director who demanded perfection in that impossible production known as my life?

Not at all. It's just that I was born with rose-colored lenses implanted in my mind's eye. Lenses that made every project look worthwhile, enjoyable, and less difficult than it turned out to be. Lenses that cast all others involved in a positive, helpful light. And no matter how many times that did not prove to be the case, I kept going.

Wouldn't having a dinner party for 12 be fun? Didn't that struggling committee have potential to develop into something grander if given a little push. Taking on more and more; each day resembling the crowded cabin scene in "A Night at the Opera" where Groucho Marx graciously welcomes one guest after another into a cramped, increasingly uninhabitable room.

My performance schedule slowed down as I reached my mid-70s; decreasing mobility and night vision limiting my performances to matinees in easily reached venues.

Until a decade later when COVID and ZOOM offered a new role—Old Woman. This character is not on the stage but in the audience. She does not generate the action: She responds to the actions of others.

Many people want to show me their acts. Some remember me from previous shows, or have recently come to know me, or just heard about me from someone and decided to get in touch. They welcome me into their worlds each world expanding my own.

My peers are few in number and dwindling fast. We are audiences for each other. A few of us are "still active" but definitely winding down. Yet, just checking in with one or another of them makes my day.

Then there are those in their 40s, 50s, 60s—my children and their friends the children of friends who have died. Some I remember from a time before they remember themselves. Others came into my orbit when they were in their teens. They are joined by former students, new and old colleagues. And magically, millennials—my granddaughters and a few mentees I have picked up along the way.

How busy they all are! I sit in silent awe of their accomplishments, their projects. Until something they are doing reminds me of something I once did. Or of a person they should meet, a resource to pursue, a few words of advice

And I can help.

Freed from the expectation to do, I can simply be. I clap loudly. I call Bravo and Brava. I pull myself up from my seat to a standing ovation, then walk over to the couch, lie down, and take a nap. It is all anyone wants or expects from me. All I want or expect from myself. Old Woman is the role of a lifetime.

STILL LIFE WITH FRUIT

Bananas. Avocados. The very names exude health. Their shapes and colors o pleasing to the eye. I felt virtuous as I placed them in the supermarket art, on the price scanner at check out, pulled them four blocks home in my hopping cart, placed them in a handmade ceramic bowl, and set them on the enter of the kitchen counter.

They were ripe and ready. I was not. Firm and vibrant when they entered is room, they lived up to their promise. I did not. They weigh heavily on the ind. I could make an avocado smoothie. Or a banana bread. Or a lot of ther things—each involving additional ingredients that appeal to my appe- te no more than these bruised, shriveled specimens before me.

This is not a rare occurrence. In fact, the burden is magnified when the de- aying produce is seasonal bounty from the Union Square Farmer's Market. wander back and forth among its booths, transfixed by at the abundance nd variety, stopping to note with interest the arrival of corn, the departure f potatoes.

Day before yesterday, a bunch of broccoli rabe called out to me. How could not bring it home, sauté with garlic and red pepper flakes, and enjoy that ery night? Today the remaining half of the bunch rests in my fridge, nestled gainst a softening cucumber I do not want to sauté, pulse, chop, whip, or ombine with anything else. I've had my fill.

The broccoli rabe will remain there—a blight on my spirit, a weight on my eart—for the next week. I will approach it a few times with great intentions. erhaps I could make....? No, this is not their night. Maybe tomorrow?

Of all the injustices in the world, the country, this city—hunger troubles me e most, is the recipient of the lion's share of my charitable contributions. et I waste, regret, and waste again.

Removing the evidence of my crime is a surreptitious business—even ough no one is watching but my conscience. Under the eyes of the "starving rmenians," I was urged to remember in my childhood the billions of hungry eople who occupy this planet, this block, with me. I place the food rejects astily into the garbage bin, twist the top, and doom them to destruction and yself to lasting guilt.

EARLY SUNDAY MORNING

I arrive at yoga class half an hour early to secure my spot on the far right of the last row. I have wiped down my mat and two blocks. They—along with the water bottle, the folded blanket and two towels—are carefully arranged about me.

No one notices me here. I can see everyone, watch them filing in, each involved in a ritual of preparation. Young women, one or two young men; all at least 40 years younger than I. I admire their grace and ease, wonder at their tattoos and piercings, appreciate their diversity of size and shape. Here again today is the short, compact Asian woman and the tall Dominican with the perfect posture. And whoa—another old lady! Well, relatively speaking. She is probably in her 60s but look at her go. She is warming up by standing on her head.

This is not a competition, I remind myself. So what if some of the poses are so difficult I don't even try; that my attempts at others are clumsy at best, grotesque at worst? I have my moments. The times that I bend and reach in rhythm with the others. I am a candy in the box, a chip in the mosaic, a spoke in the wheel, a part of this group of strangers who have come from all parts of the world, to be here, in this room, together.

We have five breaths for each pose. Five breaths take longer than you would think. (Breathe In, Breathe Out—Breathe In, Breathe Out—Breathe In, Breathe Out—Breathe In, Breathe Out—Breathe In, Breathe Out)

Here comes my favorite. Legs folded, shoulders back as far as my scoliotic back allows, achy right arm joins the limber left arm, my hands meet in prayer behind my back. I am on a mountain top in Tibet, I am at peace, at one with the universe, I Am the Buddhist nun.

THE SCARLET LETTER

I wanted to look my best. Knowing that the examination would require avy blue paper shorts, I chose a snowy white sweater to set them off, pearl utton earrings that (since my teenage ears were pierced 65 years ago) I'd een led to believe were Just The Thing to enhance winter white.

In the waiting room was a wondrous though complex coffee machine and—vith just a bit of help from the receptionist—I was able to secure French va-illa and carry it with me into the consulting room. Slacks off, shorts on, flats overing my gnarled toes, I sipped as I awaited the orthopedic surgeon.

Time passed slowly, but contentedly. I thought I looked quite fetching and ne coffee was good. Until, oh my, a drop spilled on my sweater. There was a ink and paper towels, so I splashed and swabbed until the brown spot turned an. At which moment, four people entered the room: surgeon, resident, med-al student, nurse.

I had rehearsed my role—not just the lines but the deep understanding that nforms them. The motivation of each of the actors. How to project the im-ge that best reflects my character: mental acuity, wit and spirit, information had accrued from extensive research on the web.

The surgeon—a practiced blend of authority and empathy—was fit for rime time. The resident nodded. The medical student stared. The nurse took otes. It was my turn; the memorized questions affected calm in the face of ar.

But then, there was the tan spot. Was I just imagining it or were everyone's yes drawn to it as I spoke? Not a bright, with-it old lady at all—but a rather loppy one; a host of hidden physical and cognitive problems revealed.

After that moment I took little in, gave little out. I was only biding time ntil I could get to the ladies' room where—with soap and vigorous scrub-ing—the spot completely disappeared. Too late to make a difference. A mall incident but I couldn't get it out of my mind. I flashed on an image of Iester Prynne forced to wear a Scarlet A on her bosom so that the shame of er adultery would always be before the crowd. That was it. I was ashamed.

A young person can splash herself, make a stain, laugh it off. The same stain in old age hints at global incapacity. The shame of the old in soiling themselves is akin to the shame the child feels for having "an accident." "They will call me a baby" morphing into "They will think me senile." Strange that I had accepted signs of aging in my appearance and in my health but the sense that I might be seen as less than capable to care for myself struck a nerve.

* * *

I returned to *The Scarlet Letter* after a hiatus of 60 years to find that had forgotten the ending. Hester's lover, Reverend Dimmesdale, wastes away from guilt until he confesses and dies at peace. Hester's husband, Roger Chillingworth, seeks revenge and dies an ignoble death. Comfort in the release of a painful secret and the self-destruction inherent in seeking retribution are obvious lessons of this fable. But what to make of Hester, who—after years of living in the wider world—decides to return to Salem, takes up the scarlet letter, and wears it until her death?

When first compelled to wear the letter announcing her downfall, Hester creates a work of art. The beauty and opulence of the letter is echoed in the gorgeous clothes she contrives for her daughter Pearl. Their garments give out a glow, set off in bold relief from those of the settlers whose dark, drab clothing reflects the dark drabness of their lives. Time passes. Hester is freed, lives abroad, returns to find many have forgotten or never heard her story. The good works that mark her life and the letter she wears have become one.

I remember my shock at first hearing the expression "crip power" and the chant "we're here, we're queer, get used to it." Words once used to shame transformed to emblems of pride? Then I remember my reaction to the coffee stain. So conditioned was I to the attribution of senility to my fumble that had taken the shame into myself.

I think of fictional Hester and her real-life descendants who turned symbol and words of oppression into affirmations of their identity and worth. They grasped an essential truth: Claim your humanity from those who would deny it and you are free. I will try to do the same.

CAMEO PERFORMANCES

At Yoga.
It was my first time in the 1:00 pm Wednesday class. All the students appeared to be under 30—as was the teacher. I felt her eyes on me throughout the hour. As I rolled up my mat, she walked over.
She: Well, look at you!
Me: Silence (Yes, look at me.)
She: (amazed expression) You could teach the girls in the front row a thing or two.
Me. Silence (The girls in the front row are doing Swan Lake.)
She: God bless you!

At the Craft Store.
Lost in thought, I place my purchases on the counter without looking up.
She: Big plans for Halloween?
Me: What? (Stunned into attention)
She: Big plans for Halloween?
Me: No, I don't... (Do I Look like someone who would have big plans?)

At Starbucks.
I am waiting in line for a Tall Pike. the barista, turns and hands it to me.
She: Here you go, young lady.
Me: You can see I'm not a young lady. (How dare she?)

I used to be incensed when my obvious appearance as an old woman was ignored, patronized, or demeaned. Then, when I was about 80, I began to think—What is wrong with me? Here I go railing about invisibility from people who are invisible to me.

All they—and I—have to go on is what we see before us. I can see quite a lot. The young men and women are often people of color and/or have an accent that marks them as recent arrivals to the country or the city. They are making minimum wage or close to it. I can only imagine the financial, family, and other worries they have brought to work with them this day.

From these generalizations, I notice and respond to specifics. Why would someone dye her hair cobalt blue or paint her fingernails with little stars at the tips if not to be noticed? So, I do. "Wow." I say, "First time I've seen that color. Or "How do you get those stars to stay on?" She grins, pleased, and goes on to explain.

It seems that the cashiers at one supermarket seem sent from Central Casting to represent diversity—age, gender, sexual identification, size, shape, race, ethnicity. All are amazingly cheerful. "Aren't colored carrots fun?" one says as he places them in my bag. I agree and add, "Are you all naturally so friendly or do they train you." "Both." he says and then, "If you come in like this" (feigning a drooping sad sack expression) you don't get the job." We part with a laugh.

The cashiers at another market are all older African American women, their unhappiness with management is obvious (they speak to each other of it as my purchases are rung up). I can see why. There are not enough of them. One counter placed too close to the doorway through which chill winds blow. All I can do is remark that I agree with their complaints and tell the manager that a customer has noticed it too. Nothing, really. But I get a grudging smile.

And then one day—on a street far away from my neighborhood haunts—I am warmly greeted by name by a young Asian man in a well-tailored business suit. I am at a loss as he walks on. Who could he be? Pretty sure he's not a former student or colleague and…I remember. The dry cleaner! He was the son of the Korean owner. Dressed in a T shirt and jeans, he had placed little yellow dots on the stains and took payment at pickup. When, because I always forgot my ticket, I had to give my name. It all floods back. He left to go to college. And now here he is, all grown up, seems to be doing well. I resolve to tell his father about our meeting next time I'm in the store. He must be so proud of his son.

Cameo appearances are often the only face-to-face contacts I have in a day.

Each time I leave the house on an errand is a chance to burnish my performance.

I'm an extra in a cast of thousands. My brief appearance and few lines don't count for much; but they are something. They move the plot along, show the actors to each other and themselves in a new light, make the invisible, visible.

MENU AND METAPHOR

When nothing that needs doing seems worth doing, when a friend's illness seems beyond hope, when my aching shoulder signals that it can't take much more, when I remember that everyone I might call on for comfort is dead or otherwise engaged, I turn on the food programs. Not only do they provide practical advice that never fails to edify, they provide metaphors for life.

Take, for example, the matter of preparing a bowl of cold cereal; a task that a moderately advanced 4-year-old can handle with ease, a task that I have now been performing for three-quarters of a century. Think nothing to be learned? Consider this. If you put the cereal in first and pour the milk over it, the cereal grows soggy. Put the milk in first and the cereal on top—scoop from the bottom and each bite will remain crisp and delicious. And I think, it's like that with the sorrows of old age. You can't sprinkle them over the joys of life and deaden their pleasure; rather, keep them at the bottom of the bowl.

My favorite show is *Chopped*—a masterpiece of cooking and life lessons for home cooks and philosophers alike. Participating chefs introduce themselves by telling what led them to this place at this time. Their self-descriptions are usually inspirational—love for a child or parent and desire to make them proud, a triumph over poverty or addiction, an immigrant who believes in the American Dream.

They are then presented with identical baskets, each containing disparate ingredients from which they must construct a meal. The juxtaposition of ingredients is laughable even disgusting jellybeans in the main course basket, tuna fish for dessert. Even with a standby refrigerator and pantry to draw on, the feat seems impossible. What in the world can possibly be made of the basket (or as I have come to see it, the life) they have been handed?

What do they do with a large, unwieldy piece of something? Cut it into small pieces for easier handling. They walk to the fridge and pantry with purpose—calling on ingredients that have worked for them in other dishes (other times of life) to come to their aid now.

Flavors too strong or too bland? Balance them out with their opposites; and remember those herbs and spices (not too much, and only at the right time) that make the dish—as the life—uniquely yours.

As important as the dish itself is its presentation. Is it a pleasing balance of colors and shapes with that touch of green (parsley or chives the usual choice) to give it "freshness?" And I think of how I have seen promising projects fail because they are presented poorly. Or how the well-placed fillip can exalt a mediocre plan and propel it into action.

The judges, unlike the judges of life, are unfailingly kind. They resemble the best of parents and mentors, applauding a creative risk even when it goes awry. They recognize and appreciate the smallest signs of talent before citing criticisms. So gentle are their words that even those who are eliminated first leave with belief in themselves and a desire to try again.

The show abounds in showmanship. A race against the clock, commercial breaks timed to intensify suspense. And yet I never feel manipulated, always snapping off the remote in better spirits than when I turned it on.

MOVING TO

NAMING/SHAMING

When I started out as a gerontological social worker in the 1960s, the theory of the day (based on Erik Erikson's extension of Freud) was that human life is a series of eight developmental stages, each with a task to be mastered. The task of Old Age (from 65– Death) was achieving "ego integrity" through "acceptance of one's one and only life cycle as something that had to be." Erikson's theory had a powerful explanatory effect. (So that was why old people talked so often about the past!) It also paved the way for individual and group interventions that encouraged reminiscence such as Life Review and Reminisence.

Old age was generally accepted as a time of loss. We saw loss of loved ones in the sad eyes of this old woman. We saw loss of health and hope in the bent torso of that old man. We saw our jobs as providing emotional support and concrete services but really there was little else to be done. It was the way of all flesh.

By the mid-1970s, loss found a mate—adaptation. "Loss and Adaptation" strolled proudly together through academic books and journals. Families and friends might sicken or die. Physical and cognitive capacities might wane but the aged need not despair. New relationships and activities could fill the gaps left by those who were gone, assistive devices could substitute for what was no longer working within. Old people were granted agency over their care, and those offering it learned to be attuned to strengths as well as deficits.

By the 1990s, "Adaptation" had broken free of its attachment to "Loss" and teamed up with "Coping." So accepted were "Adaptation and Coping" that one had to search deep within professional writings to find "Loss" the problem for which they were seen as a solution.

It would seem that nothing could beat the power of "Adaptation and Coping" "until the 2000s when a cheerier cousin "Resilience" burst forth and left them in the dust. We now read of "Resilience" as the desired response to loss.

That did not satisfy the branding enthusiasts. They needed a name for the state of these resilient beings. Top contenders of the moment are "Successful

Aging" and "Productive Aging"—though it is likely that ever more inspiring names will take their place before long; so deep is the need to deny the essential facts of life recognized by poets, artists, and philosophers since the beginning of recorded time.

* * *

As of this writing, I could be cited as Exhibit A of geriatric resilience, a poster child of Successful and Productive Aging. Blessed with a modicum of physical and cognitive ability I continue to live a pared-down version of earlier days. Equally blessed with a facility for relationships, I have welcomed many new people into my life. No one sees the days I feel overcome by the loss of irreplaceable loved ones and the effort of keeping myself functioning from morning to night.

Since reaching my 80s I seem to have an incident a day. Nothing major— just something to remind me that my reflexes are slowing, my senses are fading, my digestive system has taken on an unpredictable rhythm. I go to place a jar in the pantry, and it falls from my grasp. I search out the restroom as soon as I enter an unfamiliar space. I sit down to read and awake half an hour later with the book on the floor. Conserving energy for projects that mean the most to me, I limit activities (and some days, taking a shower counts as an activity). My skin is so dry it sometimes tears, so thin that black and blue spots appear at the slightest bump. The smallest household tasks take longer and are more tiring than I could have imagined. Yet aside from a few manageable chronic conditions, my doctor pronounces me quite fit.

I am not alone in this. Others who have lived long enough to feel the effects of a thinning world and waning capacities understand. We do not seek resilience but meaning and purpose in our extended lives, assurance of acceptance and support when we need it.

Resilience cheerleaders would have us believe that we can will it into being; that a healthy diet, regular exercise, social interaction, and a positive outlook are all it takes. They have nothing to say about old people who are at the mercy of their genetic inheritance, poor medical care, insufficient income and social supports to meet their basic needs.

As if that were not enough. Examples of what has also come to be known as "well aging" are generic, with no recognition of old people who find individual sources of fulfillment. My television screen features advertisements of old people living joyous lives as a result of one medication or another. When not playing with adorable grandchildren, they are engaged in group or athletic activities. I have yet to see anyone reading a book, listening to music, walking about observing the world around them, cooking a creative meal for one, much less sitting and thinking. It is impossible for me to imagine a life without those solitary pleasures.

No one recognizes that the "successful" group I led last Thursday was preceded by a week of spaced-out preparatory tasks followed by an exhaustion a younger person would experience after running a 10K; that the "productive" hours spent writing this essay are bracketed by days of doing.... nothing much.

So, what if I go on this way, steadily being, doing less and less until I die? Periods of productivity will lessen. Successes will disappear. I will not be unproductive; I will not be a failure. I will just be winding down, wearing out, as my old body was programmed to do.

Cease and desist, I call out to those who sit in judgment of how we live our last years.

Age shaming may not have been not the intent of your efforts, but it is the result. The shuffling off of loss and diminishment in its place in our lives denies me and my peers the dignity and respect we deserve. Appreciate all it takes to rise each day in its presence and find pleasure in what remains. Find comfort in the hope that old, ill, or disabled as you may grow, you may still be of value in this world.

MISSING

"Missing" is a contranym—one of 75 words in the English language that hold opposite meanings. It can refer to being absent from what is present (I am missing the meeting) or to being present to what is absent (I am missing you).

Eleven years after Roy's death, both meanings of the word are alive within me. I am missing the agony of seeing his health deteriorate, the slow whittling away of the man he was. I am missing the constant worry, the fear of what will happen next. I am missing the guilt of wanting more time for myself.

Life is easier now. But oh how I am missing Roy.

July, and I miss him coming back from a sail—as sated by a day on Lake Montauk as a sailor back from the Seven Seas. October, and I miss watching him dig up the garden and bring plants into the greenhouse. December, and I miss walking through the city with him, enjoying the holiday lights. April, and I miss taking a break from work to have lunch with him at our favorite Chinese restaurant.

Any day, any month, and I miss him beside me in the bed, across from me at the table, by my side in the car. I miss being the most important person in his life. And having him be mine.

Roy's judgment, his take on life, are a part of me now. Often, I find myself responding to a situation as he would have. I miss what is gone forever: his deep voice, measured speech, big feet in big white sneakers, three tiny wrinkles in front of each ear that I don't believe anyone but me (and possibly his barber) ever noticed. His hands.

Roy had wonderful hands, the palms never sweaty, always warm and dry. Not soft lawyer hands from turning pages, shaking other soft hands. Rough workmen's hands from sawing wood, wrestling with machinery that would not do his bidding. Sometimes I would place my palm against his at the wrist, just to see my 7s against his 12s. Other times I would reach for his hand as we walked outside or sat together in a theatre, hold it for a while, let it go. He accepted the reaching as he accepted the letting go—without commenting or questioning why. It was his way in all things.

Queen Victoria had a plaster cast made of Prince Albert's hand after his death. She slept with it beside her for 40 years, taking it with her when she joined him at the Frogmore Mausoleum. The Riverside Chapel does not perform these services, so I have no such replica in my bed, or to accompany my ashes (that will be mingled with the remainder of his) for our children and grandchildren to toss to the sea in Montauk.

We agreed on the town, on the ocean, but the specific spot of the coastline was left to me. Each July—when our family goes to drop flowers and tears where Roy's ashes were cast—I congratulate myself on the choice.

It is the Easternmost tip of the United States— the spot where the sun first appears. We can see the historic Montauk Lighthouse and fishermen in the distance but here we are alone. We stand on a sandy cliff, the ambient sounds are waves breaking, gulls yapping. On a clear day, we look down and across a rocky hill to the bluest of oceans. We look up to the bluest of skies. A good place to go missing, a good place to be missed.

BECOMING WHO WE ARE

I have no more made my book than my book has made me. —Montaigne

I am the daughter of an amateur musician and the mother of a profession-al musician. I do not play, sing, or read music. I am a listener and (like that apocryphal museum goer who says, "I don't know anything about art but I know what I like.") my interest in music is rooted solely in the feelings it arouses within me.

I am particularly drawn to compositions based on a constantly repeated theme: what I have been told is called a "ground bass." The theme is simple and compelling. Variations fly up from the theme, keep it company for a while, fade away. Many of my favorite works —from Bach to Philip Glass— share this characteristic. There is comfort in the continuous thrum, surprise and pleasure in its twists and turns, satisfaction when it ends close to, but never exactly, where it began.

The essays in this collection were written in the seven years following pub-lication of *The Lioness in Winter*. Like the women authors cited there, I am a product of my time and place in history. I dip in and out of a few locales, center on a handful of recurring themes, mix past and present. With a differ-ence. My lionesses wrote because writing was their life's work, a continua-tion of all that they had been and done before. Years of converting inchoate thoughts and feelings to words on a page served them well as they wrote on into old age.

Pick up any page of Colette and know it could not have been written by anyone else. It is her ground bass. Its steady thrum is loud and clear in each subject she turns her attention to and what aspects of it she finds of note. The same might be said of the other famed authors whose late-life works are meaningful to me.

I am a social worker by trade, and at heart. All my previous writing was generated by the desire to share knowledge with others. Whether it was pre-senting concepts and intervention strategies to a professional audience or introducing useful findings of memoir to a general audience, I was a strict censor of my own life. Even *The Lioness in Winter*, a most personal work, was written to the expectations of an academic press.

I had not yet found my ground bass. Reading over these essays makes me newly visible to myself. I note the repetitions of some themes, the absence of others, tics of phrasing, and attitudes with deep roots. I have written myself into being.

Montaigne, whose famous quote heads this chapter, is credited with being the first essayist. A 16th-century nobleman whose life and works were superbly summarized by Jane Kramer ("Me, Myself, and I," *The New Yorker*, August 2009), he created a literary genre. No one before him had created a character called "myself." Montaigne's mind led, his pen followed; a stream of consciousness that lit on a theme, explored, it, moved on. Not autobiographical or confessional, simply a record of all that filled his being at the moment he sat down to write.

No Montaigne am I. I contrast his image (goose quill pen in hand, looking out from a tower on his Bordeaux estate to the vast lands beyond) with mine (a windowless closet/office barely large enough to hold computer, printer, and chair) and laugh. I think of his works (wisdom that has proved generative to scores of readers and writers in the centuries since his birth) and sigh. Yet our impulse, our method, is the same.

It goes like this: A theme presents itself, my mind threads through it for days. I think of it when I am out for a walk, cooking dinner, taking a shower. No, this is close to what I think but not totally. Why had I not considered that? The past pops up when I least expect it. Quotes from what I have read brush up against an impression of a moment ago. I know as I write that my thoughts will change, are indeed changing as I see the letters, the words, the sentences form paragraphs on the page.

This book is not my creation. It has created me. Writing is an act of discovery and recognition of how much I am like—and unlike—any other old woman who might leaf through its pages. And that of her daughters and granddaughters who might be seeing their own futures as they read along with her.

Dear Reader: Are you a woman in your 60s, 70s, 80s, 90s? What is your story?

Tell me about the joy you find in nature, the love you feel for your cat, your dog. What is it like to live off the grid miles from the nearest house, or in the same small town or community in which you were born? How does it feel to be struggling with poverty, with racial prejudice, with language barriers in a country in which you have just landed after a life of horrors somewhere else?

How has being lesbian or bi-sexual in a time when such identity was devalued affected your old age? And so much I don't even have the imagination to wonder about and yet are important for me, for those who come after us. to read. What is your ground bass?

Your stories would not only open the speakers and writers to a new understanding and appreciation of their own lives, but they would also expand the world's understanding of the trials and possibilities life holds for old women.

Bertha Reynolds, (a social work theoretician equally influenced by Freud and Marx) alerted the profession to the importance of moving from case to cause, from the individual to the community. In so doing she preceded one of Gloria Steinem's major contributions to Second Wave Feminism: The idea that we learn and grow most through sharing our stories and identifying common themes on which to act.

What would happen if "the personal is political" of consciousness raising groups of the 70s were moved ahead 50 years? If second-generation feminists and those who come after them take up the subject of old age as they move into its orbit?

The lived experience of women was invisible until the Baby Boomers came along. I struggled with juggling the demands of job and family long before accounts of how to achieve "Work/Life Balance" began appearing in popular discourse. I was in misery and made my family miserable for a few days every month until I learned from them that it had a name— "PMS" —and there were better ways than mine to deal with it.

Writing one's memoirs has long been seen as a respectable pastime for elders, and many senior centers and facilities foster such groups. A legacy to one's family, to the collective memory of one's community is a worthwhile goal but falls short of its potential for writers and readers. A memoir is a story of a life that is passed, not a life that is still going on.

The 60-year-old woman of today has a life expectancy of 23 years. Even , at 85, may well live six more years—far from a sure thing (as if anything s). She is most likely to be touched by grievous losses (the fears that haunt our nights) but just as likely to have moments of discovery, of joy (flashes of which we can experience any day) that need to be written about and heard.

The women who shared their experiences, and so changed the world, are now entering their 70s. A time when the skies darken, when they will look around for guides, and find few. Will they remember how they stood up and spoke out for each period of their lives as they went through it, and pick up that mantle again to write it? I have hope that the following blank pages will be filled by You.

CPSIA information can be obtained
at www.ICGtesting.com
Printed in the USA
LVHW040247240822
726654LV00009B/825

9 798218 032920